THE EARLY YEARS
THE 1932–1946 LETTERS

Joel S. Goldsmith

I-Level
Acropolis Books, Publisher
Lakewood, CO

THE EARLY YEARS
THE 1932–1946 LETTERS

First Acropolis Books Edition 1998
© 1949 by Joel S. Goldsmith

All Bible quotations are taken from THE KING JAMES VERSION

For information contact:

Acropolis Books, Inc.
Lakewood, Colorado

http://www.acropolisbooks.com

Library Of Congress Cataloging-in-Publication Data

Goldsmith, Joel S.,   1892–1964.
    [Correspondence. Selections]
    The early years: the 1932–1946 letters / Joel S. Goldsmith.
        p.   cm.
    Previously published: The letters. Marina del Ray, Calif. :
DeVorss & Co., 1949
    Includes bibliographical references.
    ISBN 1- 889051- 33 - 0 (hardcover : alk. paper)
    ISBN 1- 889051- 34 - 9 (paperback : alk. paper)
    1.Goldsmith, Joel S., 1892 – 1964 -- Correspondence. 2. Christian Science.
3. Spiritual Life.   I. Title.
    BP610.G641555   1998
    299' .93–dc21   98-12365
    [B]   CIP

This book is printed on acid free paper that meets the American National
Standards Institute Z 39.48 Standard

Except the Lord build the house,
they labour in vain that build it. . . .
                                    –Psalm 127

"Illumination dissolves all material ties and binds
men together with the golden chains of spiritual
understanding; it acknowledges only the leader-
ship of the Christ; it has no ritual or rule but the
divine, impersonal universal Love; no other
worship than the inner Flame that is ever lit at the
shrine of Spirit. This union is the free state of
spiritual brotherhood. The only restraint is the
discipline of Soul; therefore, we know liberty
without license; we are a united universe without
physical limits, a divine service to God without
ceremony or creed. The illumined walk without
fear–by Grace."

                    –*The Infinite Way* by Joel S. Goldsmith

TABLE OF CONTENTS

TABLE OF CONTENTS

TABLE OF CONTENTS

AUTHOR'S NOTE

My original introduction into the world of metaphysics was through the study of Christian Science. For sixteen joyous years I was a Journal practitioner, during which time I served in many positions in branch church work, including that of Board Member, Chairman of many committees, nearly two years as First Reader of Christian Science services in Riker Island Prison, New York, another year as a member of the Committee of Christian Science Activities at Norfolk Colony Prison, Massachusetts, serving also as substitute Reader there, and a full three year term as First Reader in a branch church in Boston, Massachusetts. Because my practice quickly spread throughout the United States and many foreign countries, a large correspondence was necessary, and often requests came to me to continue sending letters to patients who had been healed but desired further enlightenment. It was in this way that the idea of writing a weekly letter unfolded and for many years this practice was continued. These Letters do not constitute an attempt to teach Christian Science; they merely present the unfoldment of this subject as it came to me as an individual practitioner. The understanding of this approach enabled me to operate successfully as a Christian Science practitioner, and the reason for publishing these Letters now is that this volume may serve to help students who have not yet found a foundation upon which to build the greater awareness of God. To metaphysicians who have not followed the Christian

Science teaching, this book will also be a help, because it presents the foundational stones upon which the superstructure of truth and love may be built in consciousness.

It is upon this foundation of God as the only cause and creative principle that my consciousness has unfolded to the degree now shown forth in my later writings: *The Infinite Way, Spiritual Interpretation of Scripture, Metaphysical Notes, First San Francisco Lecture Series, Second San Francisco Lecture Series,* and *Consciousness Unfolding.*

I am no longer a member of the Christian Science Organization, having resigned from branch church and The Mother Church, after which my first book, *The Infinite Way,* was published. In answer to many questions from members of Christian Science Churches, I would like to say that bondage is not *in* organization, and freedom is not *outside* of organization. Bondage lies in the false concept of church, and freedom rests in one's consciousness of church. One may be in an organization and be free—or be outside and be in bondage; or one may be bound and limited by organization and free when these ties are severed. Freedom is a condition of Soul—and may only be found in spirit and in truth.

Great peace and joy on the path.

— JOEL S. GOLDSMITH

PREFACE

You are about to enjoy an unusual experience. These letters were written by me to my patients in all parts of the world during the years of my healing ministry as a Christian Science Journal practitioner from 1932 to 1946. They are known as the 'Dear Friend' letters by the many students and patients who shared them. I never thought out the salutation 'Dear Friend'—it just came with the first of those who wrote me from a distance for help. In most cases when one selects a practitioner, it is because of the recognition of the spirit in the healer. Even from far distances this spirit in one is felt by those reaching out for help. This, of course, establishes a spiritual bond between a practitioner and patient—and isn't it nature then that both feel the bond of friendship?

Although you will not find the salutation, 'Dear Friend' in these pages you *will* feel the love which revealed itself as the healing truth. You will be inside the circle of friends, who for so many years have received these letters and who have so liberally shared them with their own friends, and this love will have healing power for the receptive thought.

This book reveals the foundation for the great unfoldment which later came to me in my work, and which is now unfolded in my deeper writings: *The Infinite Way, Spiritual Interpretation of Scripture*, etc.

Lovingly yours,
JOEL S. GOLDSMITH

THE INNER SELF

by Joel S. Goldsmith

'Twas in the market-place I found Thee
    sitting at the gate—
Oh man of many faces and Master of the
    Fates.
There gathered those around Thee whose
    ears were tuned to hear
The stories of the Master and the Psalms
    of yesteryear.
"Come to Me, ye heavy laden, drop thy
    burdens at My feet—
I AM strong in faith and power, drink
    this water, fear no heat.
From the noon-day glare I shade thee;
    for thy hunger, take ye bread.
Weary sore-foot traveler, rest ye here—
    My arm thy bed.
Had ye known Me—I had led thee by a way
    ye know not of,
Under palm trees, under date trees, mid
    the shading greens."
Thus the bidding of the Master to a
    feast at Bethany
To the wanderer of the desert and the
    sinner at His feet.
"Long I woo'd thee ere ye heard Me, Long
    I bade thee to the feast

Which the heavenly Father spreadeth for
the children of the East.
Have ye precious jewels to barter; have
ye oils and spices too;
Have ye slaves and pretty dancers, borne
in caravans and boats?
Merchants rich and sickly beggars, I AM
come that ye might live,
Not by bread or wine or water, but by
streams of Love divine.
Not by food or beast or fertile field,
nor yet by golden wine,
But by My Light, inspired Word, and in
My narrow Way.
I bid ye come and eat and drink and rest
that ye might live—
And live thy life abundantly as fits
thee, child of God;
And in His many mansions dwell, in
heavenly riches stay.
Ye need not toil, nor fret ye, the
Father's Life is thine—
No power can e'er disturb thee, no
tyrant's rule touch thine.
I give thee freedom to thy soul and set
thy sore limbs free—
I give thee grace to run thy race and
peace that makes thee whole."

The Early Years
The 1932–1946 Letters

~ 1 ~

THE PRINCIPLE OF CHRISTIAN SCIENCE

The time has come for inventory. Let us take stock of our understanding of Christian Science and see how far out of orthodoxy we have come. Formerly we believed in good and evil. To God was ascribed all the power of good, and to the devil, or Satan, was given all the power of evil.

Now, through the study of Christian Science, we learn that there is no devil or Satan–but do we thereby recognize that there is no evil? It is on this point that we need to see what we are understanding as fact, or truth.

It is true that we concede no power of evil to our old devil, but do we not concede this same power of evil to mortal mind, animal magnetism, hypnotism, aggressive mental suggestion, x.y.z.ism? Have we not merely changed the name of Satan and kept alive the evil propensities and powers under another name?

In *Unity of Good* 9:27 Mrs. Eddy asks:

"What is the central point of difference in my metaphysical system? This: that by knowing the unreality of disease, sin and death, you demonstrate the allness of God. This difference wholly separates my system from all others. The reality of these so-called existences I deny because they are not to be found in God, and this system is built on Him as the sole cause."

Now sit down and seriously ask yourself whether or not you have accepted this teaching of Christian Science; whether or not you are still ascribing some erroneous condition to a cause other than God. Are you transferring the evil powers of Satan to a new one called mortal mind or animal magnetism, or have you definitely seen and understood that these are merely beliefs without power, reality, law, cause or effect?

Are you still battling error, rising above evil, handling isms as if such beliefs were actual powers or causes of erroneous conditions? Or have you caught a glimpse of the beauty of the truth of Christian Science in the revelation that God, good, alone is cause and creator and, further, that "there are no effects from any other cause?"

It is not sufficient to give up the belief that the devil is the source of evil power, we must go further and give up the belief in evil itself; we must understand the revelation that God is the only presence and the only power, and all else is simply illusion. The acknowledgment and realization that all apparent evil is but illusion is sufficient to dispel its appearance.

When Jesus was faced with his most serious ordeal, he said to it, "Thou couldest have no power at all against me except it were given thee from above"[1]—and this realization on your part will meet any situation and solve any problem for you.

Why don't we think more? What ails us that we go on year after year, generation after generation, letting ourselves be destroyed by human or material power of one sort or another, when surely we know there *is* God; there *is* a spiritual power and presence capable of overcoming mortal discords of any and every nature.

Why do we stand so seemingly powerless in the presence of germs, man-made laws of theology and medicine, persecution and persecutors, tyrants and traitors, from school bullies to national leaders? Why all this when there *is* God—an infinite ever-present power of good? What must we yet learn in order that we may avail ourselves of this divine power of grace? How do we learn to avail ourselves of divine wisdom and spiritual strength?

There is but one answer. We must *know* God. Believing is not sufficient. We must *experience* God.

We cannot look to man to save man, any more than we can look to disease to destroy itself. Our hope must be in our understanding and demonstration of God. We must live the life of God and have that mind which was also in Christ Jesus.

While sitting in meditation it happened to me. For so long I had been living in two worlds—in two states of consciousness. It was a divided existence, sometimes "out there" in reality; sometimes in and of "the earth, earthy." But that day there came a transition, a complete movement into reality; a place in consciousness "behind" the world of effect. From it I looked onto the world as it appears, somewhat like seeing a stage from behind the scenes. At that moment the detachment from "this world" was complete.

This is the fruitage of spiritual desire. It reveals the truth of the revelation called Christian Science, because in this consciousness the powerlessness of all effect is revealed and all reality and cause and power is seen to be in and of God, and God is known as the reality, law, and substance of our being.

Mrs. Eddy makes two very significant statements: "It is our ignorance of God, the divine Principle, which produces apparent discord, and the right understanding of Him restores harmony;"[2] and "If God were understood instead of being merely believed, this understanding would establish health."[3]

The error of the ages is the idea of seeking God, contacting God, communing with God, praying to God; whereas, that which is seeking and praying *is* the divine consciousness breaking through and destroying finite sense. Truth is the recognition of this truth. Life, health, harmony, wholeness, joy, peace, prosperity–all these are included in the recognition, acknowledgment, and realization of this truth.

Despite the nonacceptance of this revelation, Jesus and his teachings are on the lips of mankind, because this is the revelation of truth which must remain in the thoughts of men and be kept constantly before men until its idea dawns in consciousness and sets men free–free of the belief in a selfhood apart from God.

When this Christ, truth, dawns in consciousness, error fades out and sin, disease, hate, fear, and death lose their reality in men's thoughts. This ushers in the age of immortality here and now.

Have no other life but his, no other mind; let life live itself; let mind express itself. This is self-surrender or the surrender of the self to the Self!

God is not something separate and apart from you; God is the substance, law, life, and reality of you. God is the very nature of your being. When you begin to "feel" this, you understand the life of all the saints, prophets, and revelators; you enter into that life.

Religions and philosophies have much to say *about* God. Actually they present merely their *concepts* of God, which is not God itself.

Until God is realized as the very life, mind, and Soul of one, God still remains in the realm of concept. Truth reveals God as individual mind, as your mind. It reveals the "I" of you as God, because "there is but one I, or Us."[4] God is not "out there" to be prayed to or contacted. God is the very "I", the very principle or Soul or life of your being. God, as your mind, can be trusted to express itself perfectly. Just *let*. Just *rest*. God, as your mind, "shall neither slumber nor sleep," so whether you are awake or asleep your God, your mind is ever harmoniously active.

Only spiritual consciousness reveals that there is no error. All religions and philosophies look to God to save, to heal, to do something about an erroneous condition. Only spiritual sense reveals that there is no error. Let us be sure that we are not falling into the common error of believing that Christian Science is to be used to cure disease, remove fevers or growths, restore harmony, heal lack. Let us never forget: there is no error. "As in heaven, so on earth; God is omnipotent, supreme."[5] How, then, can there be sin or sickness?

Is not our very effort to heal the stumbling block to our success in proving God's allness? Let us accept the revelation of the Christ and rest in the consciousness of one presence, one power, one life.

We are spiritual being here and now. Let us rejoice in this truth and be forever free of the belief of a selfhood apart from God.

Christian Science has been termed the Science of Christianity and is therefore the ministry of love, a revelation of peace, and the activity of the healing Christ.

The means of bringing these divine qualities to individual human experience is its science, or principle.

Being scientific, Christian Science can only be correctly practiced through strict adherence to its rules, or principles. The Science of Christ, truth, begins with the understanding of God as the only cause. Any deviation from this rule will cause delay or failure in demonstration.

Mary Baker Eddy, discoverer and founder of Christian Science, has based her teaching on the revelation of the allness of God and, therefore, the nothingness of disease, sin and death. Her Biblical authority is found in the statement, "All things were made by him; and without him was not anything made that was made,"[6] and "God saw everything that he had made, and, behold, it was very good."[7]

Christian Science, therefore, stands firmly on the Scriptural authority of the truth that God is the only cause, and it necessarily follows that since all that he made is good, there is, therefore, no evil, and anything appearing to finite sense as error can exist only as illusion, a false sense of reality.

In practical application to the problems of individual experience, it often seems difficult to adhere strictly to this principle. Disease is often painful and seems very real. Sin is ugly, and our old theological beliefs would make sin the cause of disease and poverty. In fact, some forms of mental therapy claim that hate, envy, jealousy, sensuality are the cause of erroneous states of health; that they can cause both mental and physical disease.

Mrs. Eddy has pointed to this claim of materia medica in her statement in the Christian Science textbook, *Science and Health with Key to the Scriptures,* "The procuring cause and foundation of all sickness is fear, ignorance, or sin."[8] This belief of a cause other than God is likewise found in an ancient Bible statement to the effect that the sins of the fathers shall be visited upon the children unto the third and fourth generations. That this, however, was but the concept of the writer and not a law of God is found in a later writing in Ezekiel: "What mean ye, . . . saying, The fathers have eaten sour grapes, and the children's teeth are set on edge? As I live . . . ye shall not have occasion any more to use this proverb in Israel."[9]

It must be understood that heredity is not a law, but a theological belief, and also that sin and fear are not cause, either of disease or death, but a materia medica belief built on human history and investigation, rather than on the divine truth of being.

The careful study of Mrs. Eddy's writings reveals the true law with regard to God as the only cause, and good, therefore, as the only effect. This study will reveal the impossibility of evil resulting from the action of the human mind, whether in the form of religious or medical belief, or even from the evil thoughts of individuals or groups. In *Science and Health* we read: "The human mind has no power to kill or to cure, and it has no control over God's man."[10] Also, "There is but one primal cause. Therefore there can be no effect from any other cause, and there can be no reality in aught which does not proceed from this great and only cause."[11] This gives the general idea on which we may build our treatment for our problems. More specifically Mrs. Eddy writes, "Immortal Mind is the only cause, therefore disease is neither a cause nor an effect."[12] Also, "Neither disease itself, sin, nor fear has the power to cause disease or a relapse."[13] And she confirms these completely in *Miscellaneous Writings* when, in answer to the question: "Can fear or sin bring back old beliefs of disease that have been healed by Christian Science?" she says, "Your answer is, that neither fear nor sin can bring on disease or bring back disease, since there is in reality no disease."[14]

This establishes the basic premise of the great revelation, that only God can be reckoned as cause and only good can be the effect. Along this line we may go one step further and realize that as God is good and the only cause, all creation is necessarily the complete expression of that goodness. Here it becomes clear that error in any form is not reality, was never created and therefore has no externalized existence; it expresses only in the realm of unreality or illusion, where it has neither cause nor effect, and can neither cause nor affect any activity or quality of eternal life, which is the only life of every individual.

This entire subject is handled in *No and Yes:* "Eternal harmony, perpetuity, and perfection, constitute the phenomena of being, governed by the immutable and eternal laws of God; whereas matter and human will, intellect, desire, and fear are not the creators, controllers, nor destroyers of life or its harmonies."[15]

We are always seeking for the secret of truth, the hidden truth which is to open the floodgates of supply for us. We may be seeking the supply of money or of health, but always there is something just beyond our reach which we are sure the secret of truth will open up to us.

The more effort we make, the harder we try, and the longer we struggle, the more difficult becomes our task and the less chance we have to solve our problems. The Bible does not teach that strain and stress or profound studies are required. On the contrary, the Prophet Elisha provided abundant supply and saved the widow's son from slavery by the increase of what she *already* had in her house.

Whenever we are confronted with a problem, let us ask ourselves the question: "What have we in our house?" Now, "our house" is our consciousness, so the question is: "What have we in our consciousness?" The answer to the problem and to supply is already present in consciousness, and the abundant flow must come forth from there. This takes thought away from the outer universe or the world of effect, and brings us right back to the source of all good, our own consciousness.

The attempt to add things to ourselves from the realm of effect, the outside world so-called, must meet with failure if Jesus' teaching is correct. He said "the kingdom of God is within you"[16] and also, "When ye pray, believe that ye receive them, and ye shall have them."[17] Unless we begin with the understanding that that for which we are treating is already within our consciousness, we will be seeking it in a place where it never was—outside ourselves.

We must give up the effort to demonstrate, pray or treat for things and learn rather to gain the consciousness of the presence of all good. To gain the consciousness of the presence of all good is to gain the good itself. "Seek ye first the Kingdom of God (the consciousness of good), and his righteousness; and all these things shall be added unto you."[18] This is the secret we have been seeking, namely, that the gaining of good in any form is dependent on gaining first the consciousness of good.

Should we have money, home or position which has come to us without our first having attained the consciousness of it, we may lose it, and at best we can hold on to it only with great struggle or labor. However, that which comes to us as a result of our consciousness of good will remain with us throughout eternity. In fact, this good can never be taken away from us. It is not at the mercy of man or circumstances or conditions. Neither wars, depressions nor changing forms of political economy can take from us that which has come to us because of our consciousness of it. This was the reason Jesus could say, "Destroy this temple, and in three days I (consciousness) will raise it up."[19]

Now comes the question: "How are we to acquire this consciousness of good?" See what Jesus says about this! "Take no thought for your life, what ye shall eat, or what ye shall drink; nor yet for your body what ye shall put on."[20] Whenever a need appears, whether for supply or health, instead of sitting down to "work" about it, we should refuse to entertain it in thought and hold to the consciousness of the truth that we exist as consciousness embodying all good, to which nothing can be added and from which nothing can be taken.

~2~

GOD

"Spiritual sense is a conscious, constant capacity to understand God."[1] Many have tried to "explain" God, but so far none (to my knowledge) have ever succeeded. God must be individually experienced. Because of generations of belief in material being we seem to be far removed from God, and *only* as we live in "prayer without ceasing," that is, dwelling on the thought of God, will it be possible for the experience, or revelation, of God to come to us.

Most people either believe in, or believe that there is a God, but this is far from *knowing*, far from the assurance and the *consciousness* of the *presence of God*. Spiritual sense alone reveals it, and spiritual sense is developed through the conscious dwelling in thought of God, and *what* it is, and *where* we find it. We should also dwell on the subject: What is man? We are familiar with the statement from the Greek Temple, "Know thyself." Well, close your eyes, get quiet inside, and ask yourself: "What am I?" If arms, legs, head, and brain are not me but mine, who is this possessor of the body and mind? If I think, who and what is the *thinker?* These thoughts lead to the understanding of God.

Do we think often enough of what the word "God" means to us? Not what it means to our friends or neighbors, but what it means to us! Man is the manifestation of God, and how can we know man until we know that of which he is constituted. The manifestation of God is not a mortal, a material being. God can be manifest only in its nature, character, and quality. Therefore, the attempt to heal or enrich a human cannot be the *way* to manifest God. As we dwell in thought on what the nature of divine being is, we behold man, the manifestation of divine being, and there we find the infinity, eternality, and harmony of our own being. "Therefore the world (mankind) knoweth us not, because it knew him (divine being) not."[2] God manifests itself as love, life, being; and man is that love, life, and being made manifest.

"Ye shall know the truth, and the truth shall make you free."[3] What is truth? Christ Jesus said, "I am the truth." Did this apply to person or principle? Was this truth a personal quality or condition, or was it the very principle of his being? "Whom do men say that I the Son of man am?"[4]–"Thou art the Christ, the Son of the living God."[5] A principle is being revealed for all who have ears to hear. Truth is universal, and if Jesus declared: "I am the way, the truth, and the life,"[6] this declaration is the truth about you and me. Truth is universal, impersonal, and impartial, and is therefore the truth about you and me. Then, we should *be* the truth and thereby discover that "to truth there is no error." "I am the life." Therefore, *be* the life and discover that in life there is no death. "I am the light of the world."[7] Therefore, *be* the light and learn that in light there is no darkness. Claim your true identity and *be* it.

There is but one life, one mind, one being, and this One is God. This constitutes your identity. Then, "Cease ye from man whose breath is in his nostrils"[8]– seek no longer to improve, heal, or save him, but remember that "ye must be born again" as the Christ, "the Son of the living God." In losing your life (your human sense of life) you will find yourself to be pure spiritual being, as the life and the light.

We know that there is but one being and that this One is our only being. Then, the qualities and activities of divine being are the qualities and activities of my being and of your being. This is the being referred to in, "I and my Father are one."[9] Is this not clear? "Have I been so long time with you, and yet hast thou not known me, Philip? he that hath seen me hath seen the Father."[10] Can any message be more clear or more simple? "I am the light of the world"[11] and "Ye are the light of the world."[12] Do you believe this? "Thou art the Son of the living God."[13]

~ 3 ~

THE REAL SELF

Whatever of truth we have is mind expressing *itself*, and mind always places itself where it can best serve mankind. "Christ, or the spiritual idea, appeared to human consciousness as the man Jesus."[1] This Christ is the healer. It appears to human consciousness as man or woman, but it is, nevertheless, the Christ, or spiritual idea, regardless of appearances. "Judge not according to the appearance."[2] Do *you* see?

All that I have or am is mind appearing to human consciousness as a person. This is true of all, and the recognition of this truth is your Christ and my Christ. Error claims to appear as a sick, poor, dying, sinning, ungrateful person, but it is neither person, place, nor thing; it is illusion, claim, or belief, regardless of whatever form it may seem to assume. Man is never the belief or the claimant. Therefore, man has never had a belief. That which appears as man is Christ, and is joyous, successful, harmonious, incorporeal, eternal, immortal, universal.

It is not so much the thoughts you think that will have healing power, but what ideas of mind you can become receptive to. This is the Word of God, and it will do all that you expect of it. In other words, sit quietly and listen to the "still, small voice," knowing that mind will reveal a truth which will cause even the dead to rise.

The necessary truth to bring this about is within your consciousness. It is the "Father within"; in fact, this truth is your consciousness—the consciousness that "constructs a better body" as you trust it.

In Jesus' parable of the servants and the talents given them by their master, he says, "For unto every one that hath shall be given and he shall have abundance: but from him that hath not shall be taken away even that which he hath."[3] And so it is with us, until we utilize every bit of truth we possess, we will lose even that which we believe we have. Also, from him that hath much is expected. You have learned much of truth, and if you lay it aside it will rot in your hand just as the manna, which the Hebrews of old tried to save for the next day.

Envy or jealousy will never touch us if we see that mind alone is expressing its own qualities as individual being, and that this mind is protection to its own manifestation. Keep in thought that mind is the only actor, the only thinker, the only do-er, the only be-er, and that we are the full and complete manifestation of this infinity. Begin to see that "I" am "hid with Christ in God"; "I" am invisible to human sense or sight; "'I' am in the Father and the Father in me." This "I" is untouched and unreached by human thought.

A Christian Science treatment is infinite and, once given, operates unspent until it has completed its work. Every treatment you have ever received is *now* in effect, operating in your consciousness to reveal the harmony of God's being. My Word "shall not return unto me void, but it shall accomplish that which I please, and it shall prosper *in the thing* whereto I sent it."[4] Have faith in this Word (truth). Do not think of it as something for the moment which relieves, or meets a temporary need; it is more than that: it is God made manifest—"the Word made flesh."

~

In the degree that you hold thought steadfastly to the truth that you are life eternal will you find this allness revealing itself to you. You include within your consciousness the ideas of opportunity, home, companionship, supply, income, abundance, success, as well as all other attributes of mind. Why is this true? Because all these are ideas of mind, fathered by mind, supported and sustained by mind, and you are the manifestation of this mind; you reflect and express its qualities, faculties, activities. "I can of mine own self do nothing,"[5] but I can and do manifest that which the Father is. "My Father worketh hitherto, and I work"[6]—the Father works and I manifest the activity of that work.

When error presents itself, try to think quickly that error does not exist as person or condition, but only as appearance or argument. All error exists only as appearance or argument. Study this statement carefully until you gain the consciousness of its significance. If you will constantly know that error is never person or condition; that as life you have nothing which you have not derived from God; that any so-called condition called lack, limitation, misunderstanding, discord, separation from good, is but argument and that it can be corrected by knowing the truth of man's true nature as the infinite manifestation of mind, you will soon realize your freedom. If you will realize the joy of knowing that evil does not exist as person or condition, but only as appearance or argument, you will see why I repeat this statement so often.

Christian Scientists are sometimes subject to the superstitions of human thought, or so it would seem.

This is a contradiction of the statement Paul made that "in Him we live, and move, and have our being"[7]– where human thought or its activities have no being, where nothing enters that defileth or maketh a lie. Perhaps this underlies much of your seeming difficulty. You have not consciously separated yourself from the belief that human thoughts and theories can harm you or use you or find outlet in you.

Since you are Soul you must be infinite. Then how can you be *in* anything; how can finite thought or belief touch you; how can it touch mind or the manifestation of its being? You must realize the nature and character of man, and see why and how human thought, collectively, or individually, cannot affect this infinite immortal being. How completely free you are from all limited and limiting circumstances when this is known!

Until you learn to work from the truth that "I" am complete, spiritual, free, harmonious, unreached, and unreachable by human thought, desire, will, you will be seeing pink elephants that seem horrible and real where actually only perfection exists.

~

You are spiritual and not mortal. In thinking of yourself, do not think of yourself as you appear to be, but as a God-created being. Now, what did God create? Matter? Birth? Death? Certainly not! The God-created being consists of such qualities as intelligence, integrity, loyalty, gentleness, kindness and loveliness and we express these qualities in our daily experience as we become clearer transparencies.

Man is not visible to the human eye. You cannot see, hear or reach him, because he is "hid with Christ in God" where he "lives and moves and has his being," where mortality cannot find him, or use him as a channel, target, victim, or outlet.

We are tempted to look at our so-called human selfhood and then try to doctor it up to improve, heal, change, or save it; whereas, our salvation lies in understanding the true nature and character of man in God's image and likeness. Human experience is our state of consciousness externalized; whereas, true being is Christ-consciousness expressed. Through a purified sense of life, (a sense of life from which matter has been eliminated) we realize the true or spiritual. "Human thought never projected the least portion of true being."[8] Nevertheless, as human thought loses its faith in matter, its belief in matter, its reliance on matter, we receive illumination.

The antagonism to goodness is not in man since the only man there is, is the infinite manifestation of mind. Now, because there is no antagonism to good in man, there can be no resultant effect. You can never be more nor less than perfect, and no matter what may try to obscure this from your awareness, it is, nevertheless, a fact. This is the only logical reasoning from the standpoint of absolute truth, and all efforts to prove the truth of this statement must be made from this basis.

Sometimes we are met with the claim that the "nights" bring added distress to those suffering from disease. In such a case, all you are ever called on to do is to stand on the truth as you know it. Close your eyes and see if consciousness knows any difference between the day and night. Then, if you find that consciousness does not, you can stand on the truth that there is neither day nor night to truth. Try to imagine intelligence being conscious of either day or night. Well, you are that intelligence.

After carrying an argument as far as words and understanding take you, *stand* on the truth you have declared; *let* the truth declared be your "shield and buckler." Paul says, "Watch ye, stand fast in the faith."[9] God can't do anything. Everything already is. We have to *see* this fact, and *seeing* it is all the healing there is.

If there is no man in the physical body, what difference does it make what the condition of the body seems to be? When we have thoroughly understood this, the body will not presume to be or do anything, but we will find it conforming to that state which we have accepted as a reality in our consciousness. Actually, our body is only our consciousness of it. However, we can demonstrate only that which exists as an eternal fact and this fact in absolute truth is that the perfect and normal alone is real or true.

You must know yourself as mind, as life, spirit, Soul. Mind, including within itself infinite immortality and harmony, is your *only* mind. All its qualities are embraced within you. This within-ness is the truth of being. Theology would rob you by teaching of God *and* man, of man eternally trying to reach God, or petition him. Notwithstanding, truth reveals God manifested *as* man–"I and my Father are one"[10]–and this oneness constitutes the truth of being. Within this oneness is my life, my mind, all my good. This enables us to understand the teaching of Jesus: "I am the way, the truth, the life"[11]–"I am the resurrection and the life"[12]–"I am the light of the world."[13]

⁓

There are certain basic truths that must be held in thought until they become a part of our consciousness. As consciousness becomes imbued with these truths, they rebuild the fabric of our lives, morally, physically, mentally, financially. At a certain point, it may seem to you that you know spiritual truth, but you find that it does not seem to work in material affairs. The reason? Because you are trying to make spiritual truth change or improve a material condition.

Our instructions are, "Seek ye first the Kingdom of God, and his righteousness; and all these things shall be added unto you."[14] Actually, you do not have to look at or for things. You must "look away from the body (things) into truth and love." To think spiritually and then look at matter to see if a change has taken place is to go off the track. Human conditions must be the reflection (expression) of your spiritual thinking, but you must not try to bind them together. Spirit and matter do not mix.

You see, I, as a human, may be weighted with problems, lack, and disease, but trying to remedy material conditions is not Science.

To dwell in thought on "I", my real identity or true selfhood—my Christ-Self—and to know that this "I" is self-sustaining, is complete, is of God's being, is at-one with infinite good, *is* in fact infinite good expressed, *is* infinite mind manifested, this is the truth that reveals our perfect selfhood where a distracted mortal seems to be.

Keep your vision on your true identity. Behold in truth your spiritual, incorporeal selfhood. You are a state of consciousness. It is consciousness that constitutes your being. There is nothing outside. This understanding of withinness is the truth that makes us free from the limiting senses.

As we realize that we include within our being *every* spiritual idea, such as health, harmony, activity, home, companionship, joy, peace, dominion, freedom, we cease expecting them to come from some outside source or circumstance. As we learn that these qualities constitute our being, they unfold, or manifest, in our experience. Jesus voiced it thus: "I am the way, the truth, the life"[15]—I am the resurrection and the life"[16]—"I am the bread of life"[17]—and in modern language we say the same thing when we declare that "I embody my good; I embrace within myself my joy, my supply, my home; I include within my consciousness the power of resurrection and ascension; I am constituted of eternal life and harmony." Everything starts from "I am." This constitutes the "kingdom of heaven (allness) within you." Mortals believe there is some good to be won, learned, attained. Truth reveals that man is constituted of good, and this truth realized brings the good into visibility.

The greatest thought I know when problems seem to press is this: "I am." When I can say, "I am" then I know that nothing can be added to that which I am. "I am" indicates just what it says: "I am." "I am complete, harmonious, spiritual, well, successful, joyous, free; I am about my Father's business; I am in the secret place of the most High; I am the temple of the living God; I am the expression of God's being; I am life expressed; I am love reflected; I am the manifestation of the peace and power of God; I am perfect; that which I am seeking, I am. Over and over, I reassure myself that "I am." Not trying to be something, or to get something, or to heal something, but always consciously, joyously, knowing that I am *it* here and now. I embrace within my own consciousness all good. Create your world out of "I AM."

~4~

REALITY

Christian Science understands all evil to be illusion and, necessarily, it declares human good equally without reality. It reveals that physical health is as much a belief as sickness. Likewise, material wealth is but the opposite belief of poverty.

In order, then, that we do not vacillate between the beliefs of health and sickness, wealth and poverty, friendship and friendlessness, it becomes necessary that we come into the understanding of spiritual reality. Obviously we cannot measure our progress spiritward in terms of days or years of physical freedom or amount of dollars income. The measure of our progress is determined by the degree of our understanding of spiritual values. The natural result of our spiritual progress is a greater degree of harmony in what appears as our human affairs, but when this harmony is the result of spiritual realization we find no fluctuation and no vacillation.

This spiritual, or real state of being, is exemplified in the Scriptures in such passages as, "And there shall be no night there,"[1] and the revelation of light appearing although the sun was not yet created: "Let there be light: and there was light."[2] Again in the appearance of crops before the seed is planted. In these passages we find good appearing without dependence on material aid or accompaniment. Job says, "and hangeth the earth upon nothing,"[3] again indicating spiritual power dependent on nothing tangible to human sense. Jesus fed the multitudes with a few loaves and fishes, and this so-called miracle has never been explained, nor will it ever be to human sense. That spiritual sense comprehends and can duplicate it we know, because of the frequency with which this is done by the spiritually illumined of all ages. Moses fed the multitudes and provided water; Elijah provided food and healed even death, as did the Master Christian.

Every real spiritual healing that takes place today is further proof, if proof were needed, that there is a realm of consciousness in which harmony is the natural and normal state of being. This harmony never varies and is never dependent on any processes or methods. It is the inevitable result of spiritual enlightenment—a consciousness which unfolds within us as we continue in study and meditation on the things of spirit. Let no one be discouraged if this consciousness is not quickly attained, because to most men there are generations of material sense to be discarded before the light of spiritual revelation is achieved, and these generations of finite sense are not always dropped in a season.

Our spiritual day will dawn as we faithfully live in the spiritual integrity that unfolds to us each minute. Let us live every moment in the light of the present moment—the rest will follow.

~

Occasionally we should face ourselves with some frank questions, and one of these is: Am I seeking and studying truth for the solution of my personal problems, or for the understanding and demonstration of the eternal verities as a living principle? And another question may well be: Am I seeking the Way in order to get or to give?

Most of us embark on the spiritual path in search of health, wealth or peace for ourselves or for some loved one. This is well. Without some problem unsolvable by material means, we are apt to live out a human span with no other goal than material comfort and well-being. It takes but a grain of truth to meet these problems and, because we find some measure of relief or healing or satisfaction, we are tempted to stop our spiritual journey before we have made the transition from a material sense of existence to the realization of our spiritual and real identity.

If, after all these years of study and search for God, you still have problems, you may know that the time is here for you to make the supreme effort to transcend mortal experience. If you are enjoying good health and a measure of success, it is all the more necessary that you learn whether you are experiencing ease in matter, or whether your present good is really the result of your transition into spiritual consciousness. Let us not forget that if we have not gained the spiritual consciousness of life our present good health or wealth is subject to fluctuation, chance, change and general conditions.

We cannot bring spirit and the government of mind into the world of material concepts and beliefs. Jesus clearly tells us, "My kingdom is not of this world."[4] If the reign of principle were in "this world" there would never be age, disease, tornado or flood to experience even in belief. It is only as we rise in consciousness above the level of human thought that we approach the consciousness in which "there is no night"–no evil or discord of any name or nature.

The first step in attaining this consciousness of complete freedom is in turning from the human scene; giving up the attempt or even the desire to change, correct, heal or improve the visible scene, and realizing that as the sky and ocean meeting in the distance is but an erroneous view of what actually is present, so any appearance of inharmony is but an erroneous concept of the reality everpresent.

Is it not clear why, as long as we are trying to serve some personal and material end, we do not reach the realm of spirit? How impossible it is to pull a material rabbit out of the hat of spirit. How can we hope to find a rock of material gold in the kingdom of heaven? Yet, isn't this what we too often attempt? Let us learn, even if gradually, to drop our efforts to bring spirit to material concepts and thereby gain the consciousness of life as it is in Soul.

Through the senses of Soul we are able to behold "the reality of all things brought to light."[5] It is impossible to discern our spiritual good while believing what we see and hear. We may as well believe it necessary to lift the sky from the water, or separate the car tracks in the distance as to believe that there is sin to heal, disease to remove, or any discord to correct. Harmony is. This is the truth of being: harmony is—not shall be or should be, but eternally *is*. And only spiritual sense reveals that right where the erroneous appearance claims to be, there the kingdom of God is intact.

When faced with any discordant or inharmonious condition, remember this simple law of life: harmony is—and refrain from any effort to change, heal, correct, improve or reform the erroneous appearance.

Finally, let go of that "problem." Let life reveal itself to you in all its glory. Let the divine energies possess you.

Do not live for yourself or your own good, but for those who have not yet learned their true identity. Let go of yourself and find your Self–infinite, eternal, harmonious.

Our good should come to us as "the added things" rather than through specific mental work.

When our desires are for person, place or thing, rather than for the consciousness of the presence of the Christ, we are seeking "loaves and fishes." When our earnest longing is for the understanding and realization of God, our good unfolds naturally in the form necessary to our immediate comprehension.

Seeking objects of sense is always material sense; the desire for understanding and realization is spiritual sense, in which we find everything in the nature of fulfillment. Attempting to "use" God to further material ends is misunderstanding the nature of God, spirit. "My kingdom is not of this world,"[6] yet, when we seek the kingdom of God we find all things added.

"God is not the author of mortal discords."[7] Therefore in God-consciousness–infinite individual, spiritual consciousness–there is no lack or limitation, no sin, disease or death. Error comes to us when we identify ourselves with person. Freedom comes as we recognize our true identity as mind, life.

"I have overcome the world"[8]–not rearranged it, or added to it. "All that I have is thine"[9]–not the things of the world which I have overcome, but spiritual reality is thine and always in those forms revealing the completeness of your present experience.

"Entirely separate from the belief and dream of material living, is the life divine."[10] Then any attempt or desire to heal, help, improve or change some part of this material dream would not be spiritual science. As we lift thought above the false sense of existence; as we turn away from the dream picture, we behold more and more of reality, and the reality appearing is called healing, or changed sense of life. We must not, then, tamper with the human scene, but turn completely from it. We must not expect our good from some improved human condition or increased material supply.

There is a peace which the world cannot give us, and which the world cannot take from us. This peace is not dependent on person, circumstance or condition; it is not at the mercy of men or of money; it is the peace that springs from the infinite depths of our being. Where I am, God is—that is enough to know.

We, as metaphysicians, are not concerned with the world of effect, but with the realm of cause. We are not playing with dream pictures, but we are discovering our God-being, and looking out upon the universe as mind, life.

As person, we experience the good and the ill of persons, because person contains within itself the seed of its own destruction. As mind, life, the thoughts and beliefs and trials of the world do not touch us.

Every morning establish afresh in your own consciousness the realization of your true identity and your oneness with every spiritual idea. You are one with every spiritual quality, activity and idea. "All that I have is thine."[11] This realization brings the peace that the world cannot give and the world cannot take away.

~5~

TRUE IDENTITY

Our most important need is the constant reminder of our true identity. Only as we live in the consciousness that "I and my Father are one"[1] can we receive the continuous unfoldment of good. We must always be alert to the truth that there is not God *and* man, because there is but *one* life and *one* mind. This life and mind, which is God, is your life and mind, so it cannot be two.

All discord and disease has its origin in the belief that we have a mind and life separate and apart from God. There is but one.

We must remember that there is no law or power acting upon us, but that we are the law unto our body, business, home, supply. We have dominion over all that is in the sky, on the earth and under the water. We are the law unto it, whatever its name or nature. We exist as consciousness, embodying within ourselves every idea in the universe, and every idea is subject to and controlled by the consciousness in which it exists–not by "taking thought," but through the unlabored energy of mind, life, forever expressing itself.

It follows that the allness of God, good, eliminates the possibility of evil in person, place, thing or circumstance, and any appearance of evil is but illusion. When the drunkard is awakened to the realization that his snakes exist only as illusion, he is healed, but as long as he thinks of them as something actual, he will want to get rid of them. Rid of what? Nothing–appearing as snakes. When we realize that all disease exists as illusion only, we are healed (and one heals others), because we no longer try to get rid of a condition which does not exist.

Mrs. Eddy once asked: if a patient came to you telling you they had feathers growing all over the body, would you give a treatment to remove the feathers, or would you waken your patient to see that they never had any feathers? This is our cue in healing. Be not concerned for what condition the patient claims to have. Awaken them to their true identity, and they will then see they never had "feathers"–cancers, germs, nerves, or what-nots–but that these were only illusion, or a false sense of reality.

Our work is to live constantly in the consciousness that disease has no power. Our resistance to disease brings on the pain and even death. The disease of itself is powerless, as we have proven in seventy years of metaphysical healing. The evil power is never in the disease, or the condition itself, but always in the false universal concept or individual acceptance of the condition. Keep uppermost in thought that no disease, or other condition, of itself has power for evil. All power, the only power, the ever-present power is life, mind, truth, ever expressing itself, even where error seems to be.

Finally, the vital thing: gaining the spiritual sense of existence. It is simple to learn the letter when it is properly presented, but it takes practice and proof to gain the spiritual consciousness of truth. We do not go quickly from material sense or the intellectual knowl-edge of truth to spiritual realization. Our whole work is

growing out of mortal sense into immortal consciousness, and this entails "dying daily" to material beliefs;
"being reborn" into spiritual sense; and all this through
"praying without ceasing."

⌒

Christ is our incorporeal existence. The manifestation
of the Christ in individual experience is proportionate to
our conscious awareness of incorporeal being.

True being is eternal and independent of corporeality. It is the corporeal sense of existence that must
disappear so that Christ, our true life, may appear.
Perhaps it would be better stated to say, that as our
incorporeal sense of existence becomes more real to us,
the corporeal sense of life and body disappears.

"When Christ, who is our life, shall appear, then shall
ye also appear with him in glory."[2]

The conscious realization of our true being and of the
incorporeality of our true body is the dawning of the
Christ in individual consciousness. The light of this truth
floods our being and reveals the true Self and the
eternal, harmonious body.

Included in the human sense of life is a physical body
continually in need of regeneration, healing and building
up; also a soul that needs to be saved. Neither of these
beliefs have a particle of truth in them.

Daniel said that no harm had come to him from the
lions because "innocency was found in me,"[3] and Jesus
said, "the prince of this world cometh, and hath nothing
in me."[4] We must realize our true identity in which
"innocency" (and *only* innocency) is found, and also that
we are that being in whom error "hath nothing." This
true identity is the Christ and, when recognized and
acknowledged, manifests as our perfect being, in which
is no belief in matter, nor fear of corporeality.

The question is frequently asked, "How can I come into the conscious awareness of my true identity, or myself as Christ, when fear, disease or lack is continually confronting me?" The beginning of wisdom is to know that "God made all that was made" and he found it to be good. It necessarily follows that all that *is*, God made, and all that God made is good. Therefore any seemingly evil appearance, condition, or disease must be purely illusion—nothing, appearing to be something.

At first this is very difficult to believe and to understand. Faced with the appearance of a high fever we are tempted to reduce it or destroy it, but in this newer consciousness that "God made all that was made," we realize that this appearance of evil is just that—appearance only. It may be presented to us as a wasted lung, insufficient blood, lack of tissue, but here again we must remember the omnipresence of the Christ-self in its fulness, manifested as complete being, whether or not it be evident to the senses. "Judge not according to the appearance."[5] As we become familiar with the idea that "God made all that was made" and therefore all *is* good, we find it possible to look at the seeming appearance of evil and see it as mirage.

This prepares the way for the dawning of the Christ in our consciousness; the evidence in manifestation of true being; the incorporeal life and body, harmonious, perfect and eternal.

～

This is to share some of the fruitage of this work with you. One of the important questions refers to lack of healing. "Why don't I get my healing?" "Why don't I do better healing work?" "Why is my demonstration not complete?" At least one reason has become clearer than ever before. When we declare truths, they are usually in the form of: I am spiritual; I am perfect; I am rich; I am about my Father's business, etc., but all the while we are holding in thought our human identity, the false concept of ourselves. This treatment fails because we have not even declared the truth. It is not true that I, John Jones, am infinite, spiritual, perfect, rich, because the Mr. Jones here referred to is the limited sense of myself. But "I," the reality of my being; "I" the Christ of me; "I" the "expression of God's being"; "I" the image and likeness of God; "I" the I that I AM, *is* the "Christ,—the divine manifestation of God, which comes to the flesh (human concept) to destroy incarnate error."[6]

You see, in the first case, we are declaring spiritual truths about a human concept; trying to raise the mortal concept up to the spiritual level, which will not work. In *Miscellaneous Writings* Mrs. Eddy reveals: "Self-renunciation of all that constitutes a so-called material man, and the acknowledgment and achievement of his spiritual identity as the child of God, is Science that opens the very flood-gates of heaven."[7] Not by calling a material selfhood spiritual, but by knowing that the so-called material selfhood is no part of us and claiming only the one "I" as the reality of our being, the law unto our individual experience.

"I" in my true identity am infinite in being and expression. "I" am "hid with Christ in God," where human beliefs, mortal concepts, material laws cannot reach and therefore can have no influence; are never cause and can have no effect. "I," the reality of my self, am the "compound idea of infinite Spirit; the spiritual image and likeness of God; the full representation of Mind."[8] Therefore, "I" am complete, perfect, harmonious.

We must learn through constant effort to get close to the "I" that I am. A hundred times a day some suggestion will come about our human selfhood, and a hundred and one times we must meet this suggestion with the conscious understanding and declaration that only that which is infinite, eternal, spiritual is true of us, of our true selfhood, and naught else can "enter to defile." For weeks, perhaps for months, we must watch what enters thought so that nothing is accepted as our true identity that is not true of God. Gradually we will become accustomed to thinking from the standpoint of perfect selfhood. In which case we cannot have a sense of "I am sick; or I am lonesome; or I am discouraged," because the selfhood that can be these things has been renounced so that it is no longer a part of consciousness, and whatever of sin, sickness or limitation had been a part of the human concept of ourselves has gone into nothingness with the material selfhood, and that which is true, eternal, immortal of the "I" that I now recognize myself to be, is the only manifestation and expression.

This is not a lazy man's work. It requires many weeks of conscious effort to separate the false sense of self, with its beliefs of limitations, from the real self, the only "I" that I am, until only the spiritual selfhood talks and hears; voices only truth, and hears only "a still, small voice."

~6~

NATURE OF ERROR

Since it is true, as Christian Science reveals, that all error is animal magnetism, mesmerism or hypnotism, it must be clear that the effects of error are not physical conditions, but are mental pictures, or illusion. No hypnotist ever produced an actual physical condition by mesmerism. At worst, he has produced a mental image in thought, a distorted picture. The universal mesmerism, likewise, produces only a mental image in thought, a distortion, a dream–appearing in mental image forms called sin, disease, death.

Sin, disease and death are not, then, physical conditions to be healed or corrected, but are mere images in thought and, when recognized thus as the product of mesmerism, disappear from thought, and to our sense this disappearance is called healing. Actually, no sin or disease has been healed or reproved since none was ever there. The recognition that the so-called condition was but the mental illusion or thought form caused by mesmerism or universal ignorance is the dispeller of the dream, or actual healer.

Inasmuch as the human form, as we behold it, is not the permanent, perfect form of spirit, it too must be understood as the product of animal magnetism so that even when enjoying what is known as physical health, we understand that it is not spiritual reality. When thus understood we are able to rise above both the sense of health and the sense of disease to the apprehension of the divine idea of spiritual harmony, a harmony which never fluctuates and is never dependent on so-called material laws or conditions.

From this point on it is more clearly seen that the phenomenal universe, as we behold it through the five physical senses, is not the reality of things, but is the finite or human concept. We are not engaged in the work of doctoring this concept of body, or improving this limited concept of the world. Our task is in rising above the concept to the realization of reality. We are not merely changing a belief of illness into a belief of health, or a belief of poverty into one of wealth. Our work lies in revealing the man of God's creating, the real or spiritual man including the universe.

The revelation of Christian Science shows forth the individual as spiritual consciousness embodying the universe of ideas. It reveals him as eternal, immortal, infinite being, embodying every divine quality. It naturally follows, then, that error, finiteness, limitation, disease and death are never any part of this creation or manifestation.

We must be watchful at all times that we do not permit our attention to become so attached to the human scene—either horrified at its errors or fascinated with its seeming good—that the mesmerism holds us in the changing beliefs of good and evil, health and disease, poverty and wealth and, ultimately, in life and death.

"Thou wilt keep him in perfect peace, whose mind is stayed on thee,"[1] and, truly as we learn to live in spiritual consciousness and keep thought above the things of earth this spiritualization of thought enables us in some degree to behold reality, in which we find unchanging harmony, beauty and peace.

~

All metaphysicians will be able to heal and to meet the problems of human existence for themselves and others when they have learned, in addition to the truth about God and his universe, the fundamental nature of that which is termed error, sin, disease, lack and death.

It is clear that God is mind, principle, Soul, spirit, and that man is the manifestation or expression of all that God is. You know, then, that as "like begets like" so God, spirit, can manifest only as spiritual being; that God, life, can express only life; that God, mind, is evident only as intelligent being; that God, principle, is the divine law of harmony to its universe. The metaphysician knows the all-inclusiveness of love enfolding and protecting the offspring of God, love.

When the realization of this truth is sufficiently clear, that which we term healing inevitably follows. However, more understanding is needed when so-called error does not readily yield, or when discordant conditions seem more tenacious, severe or serious. We must understand the nature and character of error. Merely to "deny" error, or declare sin and disease "nothingness" does very little toward solving the problem, unless one *knows* the nothingness of error and why it is nothing, and can also account for the *appearance* of this "nothingness" in forms of sin and disease.

Actually, to understand the "nothingness" of error, we must return to our basic statement, "All is infinite Mind and its infinite manifestation."[2] Accepting this statement as truth, (which has been proven in thousands of healings) it necessarily follows that, as there cannot be more than all, that which is appearing to us as error must be illusion, mirage, nothingness.

Certain it is that in a God-made, God-governed universe there can be no error. Equally certain is the fact that God has not the power to engender the capacity to sin, to be sick, or to die. Then, is it not clear that man and the universe are spiritual, infinite, eternal, harmonious?

We have started with the certainty that, "All is infinite mind and its infinite manifestation," and, yet, there appears to be something present which claims to be imperfection, limitation, sin or sickness. What is it? We have named it! It is *appearance,* not condition.

Try this when you are faced with a discordant belief: instead of trying to "remove," "rise above" or "overcome" error, or to heal disease, stand still and remember that that which appears as error is only illusion. Watch the result of this calm, clear trust in the absolute allness of God, good. You will then know that the "nothingness" is only the false sense of substance, or reality, which you have been entertaining. In this connection, study the statement: "Jesus beheld in Science the perfect man, who appeared to him where sinning mortal man appears to mortals. In this perfect man the Savior saw God's own likeness, and this correct view of man healed the sick."[3]

You will find that the false appearance of error did not fool the Master. He did not "deny" it, or call it "nothingness," but he saw "the perfect man"; he saw the complete manifestation, and even thanked God for his omnipresence *as* life, where others saw death. This true "seeing" raised the so-called dead.

We, too, must see that as there is no matter, all must be spirit; as there is no death, all must be life; as there is no sin, all must be pure; as there is no disease, all must be health and harmony, then healing will inevitably follow. And, yet, not healing but the revelation of true being in all its perfection, eternality and immortality.

Study the following from *Miscellaneous Writings,* Page 25:12-15: "Science, understood, translates matter into Mind, rejects all other theories of causation, restores the spiritual and original meaning of the Scriptures, and explains the teachings and life of our Lord." Also the following from *Christian Healing,* Page 7:8-10: "It is the language of Soul instead of the senses; it translates matter into its original language, which is mind, and gives the spiritual instead of the material signification."

~

As there is no evil, we must stop our resistance to any discord or inharmony of human existence that might confront us. As we are able to cease our resistance to these discords, they will disappear, and we are only able to do this in proportion to our realization of the spiritual nature of the universe.

The foundation for this understanding is found in *Science and Health,* page 572:20 to 573:13, where it is revealed that "the heavens and earth to one human consciousness, that consciousness which God bestows, are spiritual, while to another, the unillumined human mind, the vision is material." Since this is true, it is evident that neither heaven nor earth can contain error of any nature and that, therefore, this "unillumined human mind" is seeing error in the very place where God shines through; discord where harmony is; hate where love abounds; fear where confidence really is.

The work we have embarked on is the realization that we are infinite individual spiritual consciousness embodying within ourselves all good. This is the thread that runs through every message of truth, and until this realization comes it must be our purpose and aim.

Because you are infinite individual spiritual consciousness nothing can come to you; nothing can be added. You are already that place in consciousness through which infinity is pouring. Your so-called humanhood must be still so as to be a clear transparency through which your infinite individual self may appear, express, or reveal itself.

The past is no more. It was based on the belief that you were limited to your human environment, education, opportunity, and experience. Now we know that your only limitation is personalizing good instead of seeing your good as the good of your infinite spiritual self.

~

We cannot too often go over the ground which reminds us that error does not exist as a physical condition, but as an appearance, or mental argument, which may be refuted with the truth. This truth corrects the argument and dispels the illusion or false appearance. Never think of any condition as a physical condition which has to be changed or improved. That which appears as a physical condition is never anything but a mental argument, and the truth corrects it. Appearances may testify to error but "the reverse of error is true."

Truth is not an intellectual process but a divine revelation. When one has experienced it, there are no longer doubts. All through the ages men and women have sought truth. No doubt, Jesus sought truth for most of his thirty years, then, through revelation, he found that the truth is "the Father within," and progressed until he came to the place in consciousness that enabled him to know, "I am the truth." In other words, that which I am seeking, I am, or "I AM THAT I AM."[4] Men have sought happiness, bluebirds, the Holy Grail, but all the time they were seeking truth. They sought all over the world, and returning found it in their own yard–their own consciousness. That is where you are ultimately going to find truth: in your own consciousness. In fact, you will find that this consciousness *is* truth.

We owe it to ourselves to devote thought, time, and energy to the acquisition of truth–the truth which makes us free from the beliefs of mortal existence. When we permit our time and money and thought to be taken from this objective, we cheat ourselves. Why is this true? Because in reality you are the expression of the fulness and allness of God. Human teaching has hidden this fact for many generations, and has led us to believe that we are mortals with only age and death as ultimates of life, as the logical end to our existence. Therefore, any teaching or religion which reveals the truth of our immortality and sonship with God should be pursued until it yields its full fruitage of health, harmony, joy, peace, and dominion.

Fruitage will be multiplied only in proportion as you learn that you are God-being; that you embody your good within your consciousness. Good cannot come to you. It is already where you are. Good does not even come from God to man, because man is the very manifestation of God, or good. Only in the degree that we make this truth a part of our consciousness can we prove the infinity, the omnipresence of good. Man is not something apart from God, and good is not something which man attains, because good is a constituted part of man. "I and my Father (my good) are one."[5] This should be constantly kept in consciousness until it becomes embodied.

All error will yield to truth, as there is no material law to bind the child of God, or to limit his health. All mortal or material beliefs are illusions. They are never of man. Man is the expression of only that which *is*. Mortal mind is not man; it has no outlet, channel, mode, or means of expression. Sometimes the work must be diligently continued, but often the yielding comes quickly. The constant and continuous effort of sincerely holding in consciousness the truth of being will compel any and every form of error to loose its hold.

Why is this true? Because, actually, there is no error, and this truth does reveal itself to the receptive thought. Error is always a false appearance–false appearance about the truth. "I and my Father are one," not two. Therefore, within that oneness lies your perfection, your immortality, the harmony of your mind, body, and being. "I and my Father are one," and this oneness includes your infinite good, your perpetual life and peace and joy, and that of all men. "I and my Father are one," and in this oneness is nothing "that defileth or maketh a lie." "I and my Father are one," inseparable, indivisible, here and now. "As in heaven, so on earth" this law of God, this oneness of God and man, is supreme.

∽

"Blessed are they which do hunger and thirst after righteousness: for they shall be filled."[6] When we seek truth earnestly the way opens. Both time and money come to enable us to study truth.

The same spirit that brings about increase in supply will bring about freedom from error of any sort.

Do not make belief real by thinking about it, condemning yourself, or anyone else; do not fight it as though it were a reality. Remember it is an illusion, or myth of belief. It is not your belief, but of universal human thought. Do not struggle with it; do not fight it, but sit down quietly and turn thought to divine love. Realize that this spirit of divine love is now meeting every human need. Whenever you have a few moments to be by yourself, turn thought to Christ, the divine ideal, and feel its nearness. Do not think of error, of sin, of sickness, or discord of any kind. Just fill your thought with the presence of God and this will dispel the error.

The reason that a claim may sometimes seem worse when you work on it, is because you work on it as though it were something—something that must be overcome or destroyed. As error is not a thing or a condition, but merely a belief, it is evident that treating it as though it were something, is making a reality out of nothing.

At all times remember that you are spirit—life eternal. You do not need healing. "Man is the expression of God's being,"[7] and is harmonious, whole. On the other hand, error claims to either be man or to use him as a channel for its expression, but nevertheless, it is neither person, place, nor thing. Error is not entity nor identity. It has no outlet, no channel, victim, target, law, cause, or effect. There is one good reason why we should not fear any physical evidence of disease or discord and that is found in the assurance that "God created man in his own image,"[8] and therefore man is spiritual. That which calls itself matter, material body, or physical condition, has no existence except as mental argument or false appearance. There are no physical organs or functions in spirit. God has manifested itself as mind, and that which appears as materiality is but the human concept of that which is spiritual and eternally good.

Error claims to present itself as person, as physical condition, but it is never anything other than mental argument, appearing to human thought as matter, or material condition. Being only a mental argument it is subject to knowing, to truth. The condition is not changed, but the concept of the condition is changed or corrected, then that appears which always was.

"Christ, or the spiritual idea, appeared to human consciousness as the man Jesus."[9] So, today the Christ appears to human thought as you and me, but always it is the imperishable, indestructible Christ, the divine Son, perfect being.

The error of human belief, whether individual or collective, which claims to underlie any manifestation of disease has not the power of truth. It is, therefore, not causative and cannot produce an effect such as sin, disease, lack, limitation.

Behind every manifestation of disease or discord there is the erroneous mental concept claiming to operate in human consciousness as law or with the power or authority of law. It is of utmost importance that we realize that these erroneous mental states have not their origin in mind or intelligence. They have no principle and they are, therefore, causeless and without effect.

Let us always be alert to the nature of error. If we are not, we will be fooled by it and will find ourselves accepting as real that which is illusion, mirage, suggestion. Remember, it is never a condition, person, place or thing, but always illusion.

~7~

THE LAW

"The real jurisdiction of the world is in Mind, controlling every effect and recognizing all causation as vested in divine Mind."[1] Fruitful activity is an activity of mind; therefore, it is infinite, omnipresent, and never dependent on person or circumstance.

Whatever intelligence, education, experience we may have has been given us of God and includes the opportunity for expression. We naturally include within ourselves, within our own consciousness, right activity and the opportunity for expressing that activity. Mind and its manifestation is one. Wherever there is mind, there is manifestation for they are one. This truth corrects the belief that we are ever separate or apart from our good. We include, embody, embrace within our consciousness *all* good. "Son, thou art ever with me, and all that I have is thine."[2] Nothing can be added to or taken from us.

The one thing you must keep in thought is this: "The kingdom of God is within you."[3] Never should you look to anything or anyone for that which you seem to lack, but as soon as a need seems to become apparent, know that right then and there that which seems to be lacking exists as completed demonstration within you. As you acquire the habit of continually looking within your consciousness for the fulfillment of all needs, you will find that in a natural, normal way the fulfillment will appear. The human thought looks outside itself for peace, power, supply, but truth reveals that the divine mind is your only mind, and in this mind your completed experience is evident, and *always* as manifestation.

There is no need to pray to God for anything. He continually pours forth his bounty as all that is required for your harmonious existence. This principle, or law, prevents evil in any form from touching you. If you will constantly practice throughout the day what has been written so far (until it becomes a veritable part of your consciousness), you will very quickly see things begin to happen.

In this way you set your own consciousness to be receptive to good and you throw up a protective wall around it, preventing evil suggestions from entering. You will have to learn the true nature and character of God, who in reality is impersonal principle, or law.

Actually, we embody all our good. We do not demonstrate, get, or pray for that which the Father has bestowed on us through coexistence. We are "heirs of God, and joint-heirs with Christ"[4]–"For in him we live, and move, and have our being"[5]–where we can lack no good thing.

You are individual consciousness. This truth is a law of annihilation to every erroneous belief; it operates as a law of success to you, as God's Word of creation assuring the permanent harmony of your being and its activities. Right activity carries within itself its own method of fulfillment.

Where is the divine presence and power that meets every need for you? It is within you. It is your consciousness itself and embodies your harmonious activity or employment. This truth understood is fulfillment.

My work took me back to a statement of Judge Hill, that principle was not in its idea, but governed it. His illustration was the law of gravity, which he showed was not in the object, but governed it.

While thinking along this line, I saw a painter standing before his painting and I realized that the painting of itself could not change a line or color; that the painting of itself could not improve itself nor destroy itself; but that only the mind of the painter, acting through the law that governs art, could change any part of it.

Then I saw that every organ of the body (regardless of our concept of it) is a spiritual idea; that the body itself is a spiritual system of ideas, forming one complete body; and that it is a formation of mind, conscious-ness—an effect of life; and that there is no life or action in effect. Therefore, all causation being mind, all effect is governed by mind. I saw that the organs of the body could not change themselves, but that our consciousness (the consciousness that formed them) maintained them through spiritual law; governed them through principle; and that this very consciousness was the substance of them. Mind acts through law. Therefore, you are the law unto your body. Jesus said, "I am the resurrection" (the power or law itself). Therefore, you, as consciousness, are a law of resurrection to even what may appear as dead or dying or diseased body or organs. "Destroy this temple, and in three days I (consciousness) will raise it up"[6] (through the law of resurrection that I am).

I saw further that we are a law of alchemy, transmut-ing the dross of material beliefs into the truth of divine ideas. Even that which appears as worthless, this law transmutes into perfection. This consciousness is univer-sal divine consciousness and governs, not according to our belief or even general human belief, but according "to the pattern showed to thee in the mount."

We recognize that the principle of mathematics maintains the individuality and value of every unit throughout all time, and in this same manner the principle of music maintains the individuality and value of each note unto eternity. We also know there is a principle governing even such so-called physical manifestations as sun, moon, stars and planets.

Now if we are to recognize the government of mind or principle in the realm of the stars, numbers, and music, how much more should we recognize this principle, or government, in the realm of our body. Human belief would have God governing our body in our youth and somehow withdrawing that government in our "older" days, thereby letting the body deteriorate and ultimately die and decompose.

This belief must be overcome through the recognition that God's government is infinite and eternal. A star is never more nor less than a star; a number 2 or 3 is never more nor less than a number 2 or 3 throughout all time; and it must therefore follow that our body is just as youthful, just as vital, just as vigorous, at the end of a hundred year period as at the beginning of the hundred year period.

If only we will dwell on the infinity and eternality of God's government of the universe, we will recognize the unchanging nature of body, and all of mind's faculties and activities.

You know that there is no evil in any person, place, or thing, only in the universal concept or in the individual acceptance of evil person, place, or thing. Knowing that there is no evil in any circumstance or condition frees us from any ill effect that might come from the *belief* in evil.

We see that now so clearly in the economic theories of men and nations. As capitalism could not make all men rich, or keep those poor who would come in line with the principles of capitalism, *so neither can Nazi-ism, Socialism, Communism, or New Deal-ism make anyone rise higher than their own consciousness.*

The dependence on a power outside ourselves is always the error.

$\sim$

Down through the ages man has lost himself in mazes of belief, terming them laws, and ascribing various powers to them. As a result, he has suffered either in obedience to or violation of these self-imposed counter-feits—for most of them are laws of limitation, serving only to hinder progress and the dominion of natural birthright.

Among the harmful beliefs that operate in human consciousness as law, at least until the true nature of law is discerned, is that of heredity. In Ezekiel there is a definite promise given us: "What mean ye, that ye use this proverb concerning the land of Israel, saying, The fathers have eaten sour grapes and the children's teeth are set on edge? As I live, saith the Lord God, ye shall not have occasion any more to use this proverb in Israel."[7] In spite of this though, the beliefs persist in inherited disease and sinful habits. Many make little attempt to carve out successful lives because of the almost universal acceptance that the illnesses of the fathers will manifest in the children; that the limited opportunities of one generation will hamper the next; that weaknesses of ancestors cannot be overcome in descendants. On the other hand, too much dependence is placed on inherited ability, talents, or ancestral wealth. These are usually found to fail when any strain is placed on them.

There is no law of heredity in reality, for the entire universe is governed and protected by spiritual law alone, which emanates from the divine mind, and expresses unto all men and in all situations the fulness of its perfection.

This spiritual law is forever operative throughout the universe, contains no element of injustice, knows no delay, inertia, or reversal, but embodies every activity of divine principle. It is the law of infinite life, truth and love, maintaining the rule of principle "in earth, as it is in heaven." It is the law of mind, therefore, it is impersonal. In truth there is no lie; in the consciousness of life there is no death; in the substance of spirit there is no matter. Limitless mind creates only the full bloom of immediate perfection.

Conscious only of mind and its ideas, we lose all sense of material birth, age, or decay. Individual idea is maintained in harmonious law as a separate entity, expressing its own identity and reflecting the full maturity of mind's creation.

∼

Taught as we have been for generations that all action is *in* the body, in the various organs and functions of the body, we have become involuntary victims of that belief. It is therefore essential for us to consciously remove ourselves from the influence of such beliefs.

As God is cause, all else, including the body, is effect. As effect is always governed by its cause, it follows that effect can only express the nature and character of its cause. Then the activity of cause is seen as effect; the effect is the activity of the cause and can never be separated from it. Action always remains in cause expressed as effect. In other words, God never for a moment gives over his power of action to his creation, but expresses his harmonious action *through* his creation. Then, the various activities of the body are continuously under the jurisdiction of mind and *only* the action of mind is present as the activity of the body.

By this, we know that intelligence is not a personal possession, but the activity of mind expressed as the intelligence of man; that love is an attribute of God expressed as a quality of man; that life is the activity of God expressed as man; and, therefore, that man has no intelligence, love, or life of his own either to gain or to lose, to be well or to be ill, but that man's intelligence, love, and life are God's, which he manifests *as* man. In its true light, this is not abstract metaphysics, but is the actual fact apprehended that *all* life, action, harmony, is mind and is universally expressed as man. The continuity of all being is in mind, and therefore is impersonally expressed as its creation. Only the acceptance of the *belief* that life, strength, activity, health, are in a material body, organ, muscle, or function, can prevent us from enjoying the consciousness of eternal being.

Keep in thought that that which appears as error is illusion. This must be clear to you in order to *understand* that God is all and that there is no error. This is the omniactive law of immortality omnipresent in our consciousness, maintaining the eternality of all being, and even to that which seems to have been destroyed it declares, "in three days I will raise it up." Error is impersonal ignorance of truth. However, it claims to operate through person, making its channel a victim, and we must understand that this belief, or claim, has no reality, substance or law to enforce it.

As we all are one with God, we are all equally happy, joyous, successful, healthy, and we *know* it, the evidence notwithstanding. In mind (the only universe there is) all are faithful, loving, co-operative. Our home is the atmosphere of love, peopled with spiritual being eager to serve in patience with joy and calm, appreciation, and usefulness. Over and above all is our perfect principle, vitalizing us in our various endeavors to serve its purpose, to the end that all this may glorify the harmony of our spiritual Selfhood. This is the Father's business: expressing his love.

In this atmosphere of spiritual consciousness, all are expressing his will and enjoying his grace. "Thy will be done . . . Thine is the kingdom and the power, and the glory." Let us know that we are serving him when we are serving each other. This cannot fail to result in perfect harmony.

∽

You must open consciousness specifically to the specific good desired. Why? Because in consciousness are all the ideas of harmony of the entire universe; of all the arts and sciences; the true ideas of life, love, and beauty.

Should all these pour forth indiscriminately through every individual idea, or should they be expressed intelligently in their spiritual order? The latter, of course.

Man is a self-conscious being—a being conscious of self with the power of choice. It follows that as one turns his consciousness to the receptivity of good in a specific form, he is making way for its expression through him.

At first glance this may seem contrary to the spirit of divine Science, and lest you believe that the idea herein expressed is untested or vague theory–less than demonstrated truth–rest assured that this point has caused me more study than any phase of metaphysics, and only after definite unfoldment am I able to write of this important step.

Take the subject of supply. Many earnest students have found themselves facing conditions of lack and limitation and many, operating from the mental plane–self-treatment or treatments from practitioners–have found some measure of help through the realization of truth unfolded. But many, depending on these means, have miserably failed to alleviate their condition.

Turning to divine Science, we know the infinity and the omnipresence of good; we know the abundance of mind's supply, but because we are indifferent toward doing specific work, we have failed to find ourselves in possession of this unlimited substance. Now, let us know the reason for this. Let us understand the importance of turning consciousness to the receptivity of the specific good desired.

Let us say one wanted to write a story or play, the plot or idea of which had been unfolding in thought. Would he not sit quietly and let the entire plot and its sequence unfold to thought? If one planned to furnish a room or home, would he not turn to ideas of beauty and harmony, and in peaceful reflection, let nook, corner, window places, and centers unfold in thought, until the vision was complete?

We must do just this with the idea of universal and individual income or supply. Seek a quiet period just before retiring, or the peace of early morning, and open consciousness to the influx of divine ideas. The abundance of supply is seen in the abundance of leaves on trees in the summer. Let us rejoice in the abundance of God's gifts to man; dwell on the naturalness of the infinite beauty, substance, and life in all its variety of form, with which God has endowed the universe. Let us speak praise for the unlimited forms of good manifesting throughout the universe and in each individual experience. Let us know ourselves as being compounded of the ideas constituting the bounty of God, and realize the infinity of good inherent in us as divine beings. Let us be sure that we keep open every channel of receptivity to good by consistent and abundant giving. "Freely give." This is the open fount, the proof of our faith.

There are two fundamental laws that must be kept in thought, until they become a part of consciousness, because they meet every claim of human belief that may appear.

First: there is no action, intelligence, or life in the manifest realm. All action, intelligence, and life are in and of mind (our mind) controlling every effect. To illustrate this point, let us use the law of gravity. It never enters *into* the object that it governs, but the law, filling all space, operates *upon* any object released in space. The object itself has no power to resist the law of gravity, nor has the law of gravity the power to withhold itself from operation.

In this sense does the heart, lungs, eliminative organs, and the so-called functions, have no action or power of their own. The life, activity, and intelligence of mind (our mind) which fills all space and which is all action, operates harmoniously and impersonally upon the so-called organs and functions, maintaining them in perpetual harmony. The activity of mind (our mind) governs the action of so-called blood, nerves, organs, and functions. The life of mind (our mind) expresses the immortality of our body. The intelligence of mind (our mind) maintains the continuity of mind, body, and being without "taking thought." Therefore, we need never look to the body for harmony, health, or peace, but always remember that harmony, health, and peace are omnipresent qualities, activities, and attributes of mind (our mind) which mind expresses and which are always operating in our experience.

Second: "All is infinite Mind and its infinite manifestation, for God is All-in-all,"[8] and that which appears to human sense as error must be illusion. There simply cannot be God (all good) and error too. Therefore, it is self-evident that there is no error, and that which appears to us as error is mirage or nothingness. As we realize this truth we lose the fear of that which seemed erroneous, and normal being is revealed and experienced.

This perception of truth is the healing. Truth's universality and oneness makes healing universal, independent of personality, independent of place and independent of material conditions. For this reason, you will see that you cannot "escape" what we call healing. It lies within you not to see man as a human being with a human problem but to continue in the consciousness that man is the manifestation of God, without a problem. You have the privilege of knowing that the manifestation of God's being (man) has not a single quality, ability, or characteristic underived from its source, and therefore experiences no such beliefs as sin, disease, resentment, lack of harmony. Courage, faith, health, are qualities of God, universally expressed by man. They are ideas of which he is the compound.

Activity is of God and is therefore never failing. You are God's own selfhood made manifest. There is no personal health or wealth. Health is not any more a condition of body than wealth is condition of money. Therefore, they are omnipresent and eternal in man, who is mind's expression of itself. There is not mind *and* man, but mind expressed *as* man; spirit formed *as* man; love expressed *as* man; life revealed *as* man. Nearer and nearer we come to that state of consciousness wherein we find that mind alone governs its ideas. When we, however, look at the so-called physical organs and seek God's government in them, we are expecting to find divinity in human concepts. This is why we fail. "Think on these things."

∼

A word on "heredity": Error that is not real today could not have been real yesterday, or at any other time. That which appears as an erroneous condition was never more nor less than false appearance. There is not now, and there never was a condition of error, because God made all that was made, and *all* that he made is good.

Give daily thought to this: Error does not exist as person or condition. It is always a suggestion. Man "is the compound idea of God, including all right ideas . . . that which has not a single quality underived from Deity."[9] Then nothing erroneous can have existence as a condition of man, but exists only as appearance or argument about man.

This places error in the mental realm, where it can be corrected with the truth about man as the offspring of spirit, in the sense that spirit is his source. The argument of error has to be met in our own thought, never in the other person's thought, because it has presented itself to you and to me and we must meet it within ourselves with the truth of being; with the truth about God and man.

Disease does not belong to man, and human thought cannot use him for its expression or manifestation. Divine law is no respecter of persons. All the good of God is universally, impersonally, and impartially available to all here and now. God is life. He is the life of man, and man can no more be separated from life than four can be separated from two times two.

A falsity that we must avoid is the belief in a personal selfhood; that the compound idea of mind can express a quality, activity, or condition which another lacks. All good is God manifested equally by all. All evil is impersonal error without cause or effect. It is illusion without body, mind, substance, law or being—nothingness, nowhere, no time. Why fear that which is neither presence nor power?

Jesus was once asked: "Who did sin, this man, or his parents, that he was born blind?"[10] And he answered: "Neither hath this man sinned, nor his parents: but that the works of God should be made manifest in him."[11] He knew that error has no power or presence; no cause and therefore, lacking divine authority, it could have no effect. The divine power that made man maintains, sustains and nourishes its own image and likeness. Man's principle is divine love, which never leaves him nor forsakes him. "As I was with Moses, so I will be with thee: I will not fail thee, nor forsake thee."[12]

Know that there is but one mind, one intelligence, one life, and that you, like all men, embody this infinite wisdom in its wholeness and perfection. We are not responsible for any evil that we seem to be a channel for. Through ignorance, we have allowed these things to find us as outlets, but we can at any time stop them. We can begin with the simple truth that we are the manifestation of God's being and therefore the outlet for his qualities only—love, peace, rest, abundance, health, harmony, joy, dominion. Then remember that evil, whether in the form of sin, disease, or lack, cannot find the manifestation of God's being an outlet or victim.

∽

There are two related statements. The first: "There shall no sign be given,"[13] and the second: "These signs shall follow them that believe."[14] You will note that the "signs" (healing) "follow them that believe" (understand). This is because healing is the result (the outward sign) of the understanding of truth. No sign can ever be seen, therefore, before we reach this understanding. The "signs following" is merely the evidence to human apprehension that we have arrived at spiritual understanding.

No intelligent person would consciously cling to a phase of error and, thereby, delay or prevent healing. However, there is always one yardstick that we can use: "The Sermon on the Mount." We need frequently to ask ourselves whether or not we are making the effort to live up to this document. Human goodness is not enough, because if it were, the Ten Commandments would have sufficed. Jesus made it clear that to abstain from murder is not enough. We must not even become angry with our brother and, of course, this means that we must never be impatient or unloving; lose our temper, or get discouraged at his shortcomings, for all of these are predisposing causes toward anger.

It is not enough that we lend to those in need. We must not expect a return from that loan. We are to realize the infinite source of our supply, which never requires that we receive back that which we once give out. It is, of course, just that we accept the return of a loan, but looking for it is the error. In forgiving those who trespass against us, we understand that we are not to condone the error, but to know that as man is spiritual, he has never been guilty of wrong toward us. This, you see, is a purification of self.

As to affirmations. We sometimes seem to need these and, where it seems advisable it is wisdom to indulge them until the light is clear. It is safe to assume that *all* erring belief is in general human thought and is not your own thought. Know that you are not a channel or outlet for such, as you are the manifestation of divine mind.

Study Christian metaphysics daily until they bring forth a response within you. First of all, establish yourself on the foundation of truth. Thereby, you can learn that error is not cause and can, therefore, have no effect. When we see clearly that error is not causative, we are able to understand why there are no such effects as disease and discord.

We must have confidence in that which we have not seen. Remember Thomas? He was willing to believe what he could see and feel, but Jesus said that it was greater to believe that which the physical sense could not see. Agree that God, the divine principle of the universe, is perfect in essence and in expression, and that the law of God is universal, impersonal and impartial.

Do not make yourself weary with mental effort. Relax. Rest in the truth: I am the truth expressed; I am life manifested; I am the infinity of being, because there is but one life, one mind, one being. As "God is all-in-all" there is actually no you, no one but God. Do not fear what flesh can do to you. To believe that matter can help or hinder us is idolatry. To fear it, is also to give it power, or just another form of idol worship. There is no power but good, truth. Evil is not power. We are called on to stand fast.

~

The work of correcting discordant beliefs is always our own, within ourselves. We often try to correct the other fellow, whereas, we can correct only our own concept of the other fellow.

Do you believe you have any human relations? There is but one Father-Mother, and we all are the off-spring of that parent only. "The only begotten of the Father" shows that God has but one Son, and we all are the manifestation of that oneness.

Do you believe that someone is, or was good, kind, tender? Listen: "Why callest thou me good? there is none good, but one, that is God."[15] Do you believe that another is unkind, critical, unappreciative? Listen: "Neither hath this man sinned, nor his parents"– "Neither do I condemn thee"–"The man thou seest is the man thou beest"–"Jesus beheld in Science the perfect man"–herein is the answer to any problem.

Build for yourself a listening attitude of thought, for as we become receptive to divine ideas through "listening," we learn to reflect on that which unfolds, and the spiritual discernment of that which unfolds constitutes what we call healing. As you develop within yourself this state of calm and peace, the truth of the inner kingdom unfolding develops the consciousness of good. There is no other way to gain this consciousness. "Now are we the sons of God."[16] Do not be concerned with the intellectual interpretation of this, but try to realize that this statement indicates *your* relationship to Deity. "The letter killeth."[17]

Spiritual man does not eat, sleep, bathe, or work for a living. Spiritual man is the revelation of divine love, and that which mortals indulge as eating, sleeping, etc. is the activity of mind interpreted through finite sense. Working for a living is a mortal's idea of accepting or expressing the idea of supply. All that we are humanly conscious of is in reality the activity of mind "seen through a glass darkly." As we perform our human tasks and duties to the best of our ability, we express improved beliefs, and as we continue to express improved beliefs, we eventually see, even though dimly, a sense of reality. A higher sense of humanhood precedes the recognition of spiritual Self-hood.

You must separate yourself from the belief that you have a demonstration to make. You must hold steadfastly in thought that "I am about my Father's business" regardless of what the condition seems to be. You must cling to the truth that you do not have a single need, because you embody all your good and nothing can be added to you or taken from you. You must see with the "single" eye. Build your life in your oneness with principle and let this truth do the rest. One with God is all there is.

Where in the kingdom of God do you find a trial or a tribulation? Do you not agree that "as in heaven, so on earth" good alone exists? There are no trials because there are no mortals to experience them. We do not recognize "man whose breath is in his nostrils, for wherein is he to be accounted of?" There is only the individual whom God created in his own image and likeness, in whom "is nothing that defileth or maketh a lie"—no problem, no trial, no tribulation, no demonstration to make.

~8~

PRAYER

The essence of our work is that God *is*. We all talk about God; we think about God; we pray to God. When we realize that God is not to be prayed to, we begin to see why the talking about God is so useless, and why much of our thinking about God is fruitless.

The first point that becomes clear when we see that God *is,* is that God is not to be prayed to. If only we understood Mrs. Eddy, we would have known this long ago. Listen to her words: "God is not moved by the breath of praise to do more than he has already done, nor can the infinite do less than bestow all good, since He is unchanging wisdom and Love."[1]

"God is love. Can we ask him to be more? God is intelligence. Can we inform the infinite Mind of anything He does not already comprehend?"[2] "Asking God to *be* God is vain repetition. God is 'the same yesterday and today and forever;' and He who is immutably right will do right without being reminded of His province."[3] "Who would stand before a blackboard, and pray the principle of mathematics to solve the problem?"[4]

Then, the first step in progress is when we learn not to ask or pray to God, or expect something from him. The next step is learning to turn to the kingdom within you, which is the kingdom of God, not *for* something, but in recognition of the present perfection and harmony of all which God governs. And he governs all reality.

Also, we learn in Science that there is no evil in any person, place, or thing, but that the evil is in the universal concept of person, place, or thing. Knowing that there is no evil in any circumstance or condition frees us from ill effects that might come from the *belief* in evil.

While it is spiritual sense that meets every so-called human problem, it is nevertheless true that a conscious awareness of the truth of being results in harmony that never forsakes us, and which we consciously experience. Therefore, we must "know the truth" in order for the "truth to make us free" from those things that seem to mar or hide from us the true self of us.

If only we will dwell on the infinity and eternality of God's government of the universe, we will recognize and experience the unchanging nature of all God's creation. The dependence on a power outside ourselves is always the error.

The whole aim of our work is the realization of the presence and power of God. "I can of mine own self do nothing"[5] is literally true, but the fact remains that "the Father within, He doeth the works,"[6] rather it is the consciousness of the presence of the "Father within" that does the work. How may we become conscious of the presence of the "Father within"? By stilling the human senses and listening for the "still, small voice." I will listen for "thy voice," for the impartation must always be from mind.

∾

As we become more and more consciously at one with the universal or Christ mind, whatever desires or needs come to us, bring with them their fulfillment. As a matter of fact, we are eternally at one with this divine mind and need only to realize this truth in order to witness the fulfillment of every righteous thought and wish. Is it not clear then that man's at-one-ment with mind being established "in the beginning" through the relationship forever existing between God and his idea, man, it requires no conscious effort to bring about or to maintain. The awareness of this truth is the connecting link with divine consciousness.

As it is through the means of prayer that we attain all good, it is necessary that we thoroughly understand what prayer is and how to pray. In most orthodox churches prayer means supplication and petition to a God somewhere in heaven on behalf of some sick or sinning mortal somewhere on earth. That this so-called prayer has resulted so universally in failure to attain its ends must prove that this is not prayer, and that the God prayed to is not up there listening. Human thought eventually realized the lack of answer to such prayers and turned to a search for the true God and the right concept of prayer.

Jesus told us that "the kingdom of God is within you." Therefore, prayer must be directed within to that point in consciousness where the universal life becomes individualized as you or as me. We learn further that "In the beginning God created the heaven and the earth . . . and God saw every thing that he had made, and, behold, it was very good."[7] Being good the universe must inevitably be complete, harmonious, and perfect, so that instead of pleading for good our prayer becomes the realizing of the omnipresence of good. The higher concept, then, reveals prayer as the affirmation of good and the denial of the existence of error. When the prayer of affirmation and denial results in the use of formulas, it has a tendency to revert to old-fashioned faith prayer and, thereby, loses much potency. When, however, one's prayer consists of spontaneous and sincere affirmations of the infinity and eternality of God, good, and of the harmony and perfection of his creation, man and the universe, one is indeed, nearing the absolute of prayer, which is communion with God.

Communion with God is true efficacious prayer. It is the unfoldment in individual consciousness of his presence and power, and it makes you "every whit whole." Communion with God is in reality listening for the "still, small voice." In this communion, or prayer, no words pass from man to God, but the consciousness of the presence of God is realized as the impartation of truth and love comes from God (within) to man. It is a holy state of being, and never leaves man where it finds him.

Study "Prayer" in *The Infinite Way.*

~

We have so much of the letter of truth, let us give more thought to the spirit of truth. We know so much more of the letter than we need, and we rarely remember that the greater part is, "imbibe the spirit." The truth about this, or the truth about that, is not so important as having the consciousness of the presence of God.

"My kingdom is not of this world,"[8] because "this world" is illusion. As we "look away from the body ('this world') into truth and love" we behold God's kingdom, the realm of the real.

Orthodox religion is paganism, in that it is praying to a God which does not exist. That is why it (the church) prays and prays and yet sin, disease, death, war, and famine follow each other in steady succession. A "day of prayer" is set; the whole world prays, including its priests, ministers and rabbis, and the picture still does not change. There is no such God as is being prayed to. The prayers are going out to a void. The individuals who pray feel better because they have fulfilled a belief, but the answer to their prayer does not come.

While prayer is intended to improve or change a human condition, it must fail. True prayer is rising to the consciousness of the kingdom of God, reality–in that realm where there is nothing to be changed, healed, or corrected. True prayer brings release from physical consciousness to spiritual consciousness. It does not destroy our body, it brings us a spiritual sense of body, in which there is no discord or disease.

True prayer is developing the "listening" attitude. "The kingdom of God is within you."[9] Then, learn to listen for the "still, small voice" within you. Let the impartation be *from* mind, not *to* mind. *Prayer is the divine Word coming to us from within.*

We prepare ourselves to be true pray-ers as we learn not to concern ourselves with effects, with objects of sense, but always to look behind what the eye beholds to the infinite source of all manifestation. To lose material sense, we learn to discern that which is not visible to the outer senses. Our thought is turned more to the invisible things.

Prayer is the recognition of the truth that *all* power is God; that all power is in the invisible presence and never in anything tangible to physical sense. It is idolatry to place power in anything or any person. Each individual individualizes infinite power. True prayer is the recognition, acknowledgment, and reliance on this truth.

To what a pagan god the Christians pray! On V-E Day (Tuesday) the people were asked to go to church *next* Sunday to offer thanks to God for ending the European War! Why this thanks had to wait for next Sunday to be expressed in a church edifice is not clear. Would gratitude be less than gratitude expressed in one's home, or on the street? And why thank God for ending a war in Europe, while permitting one in Asia? And why thank God for ending a war only after the enemy is out of ammunition? And why thank God for ending a war only after eleven million Russians, five million Jews, and countless millions of French, Belgians, Dutch, British, and Americans have been killed, maimed, imprisoned, and impoverished? Where is the great credit for this achievement?

Let us watch our own thoughts carefully and see if we are not unconsciously accepting such paganistic beliefs under the guise of Christianity.

Wars and their consequences are no part of God's kingdom. Then, they do not exist as reality. God neither starts them nor stops them. God neither permits them nor forbids them. They are no part of God consciousness. Mrs. Eddy tells us that she healed a cancer that had eaten its way to the jugular vein when she saw clearly that God recognized no disease.

Wars, likewise, are but the products of a nearly universal mesmerism and cannot, therefore, exist as actual conditions, but merely as mental images of thought or distortions of fact. The end of war will come with the beginning of the realization of the nature of error as mesmerism, resulting not in conditions, but in pictures or the Adam dream.

It is paganistic to look to a deific power to remove that which has no actual existence. It is heathenish to pray to God to do God's work of maintaining his own universe. It is ignorance in an acute form to thank God for ending war after half the world lies in ruins and forty million people have been killed or maimed. If this is an actual condition, then, there is no God. But spiritual sense reveals God is, and therefore there has never been a lapse from eternal harmony and peace. Immortality is the truth. Therefore, there has never been even one death in the entire history of the universe.

Look beyond the scene produced by animal magnetism or the universal mesmerism and you find God's universe intact, and every individual safe and at peace in the harmony of his Soul.

~9~

The Mind of Christ Jesus

Our task now will be the revelation of the consciousness of the statement, "Let this mind be in you, which was also in Christ Jesus."[1] Throughout all recorded history, no such works were ever done as those of the Master and, yet, he said, "I can of mine own self do nothing,"[2] and again, "Why callest thou me good? there is none good but one, that is, God."[3] It is agreed by all students of metaphysics that the mighty works were the direct activity of that mind which was in Christ Jesus and, according to his own word, that mind was not personal to Jesus, but was "my Father and your Father"–the universal mind or creative principle of all men. Thus, the mind of man is the creative principle of the universe.

We, however, long taught to believe that our mind is personal to us, that therefore the mind of one individual differs in intelligence and understanding from another, have lost the consciousness of the infinity of mind, our mind. We can regain this true consciousness of mind only in the degree that we perceive the universality and oneness of mind.

We often hear it said, "Oh, if Jesus were only on earth today." Whereas, we must realize that the mind which was in Christ Jesus, the consciousness which healed the sick, fed the multitudes, and raised the dead, is your

mind and my mind, and in proportion as we gain
spiritually this perception, will we do those works, "and
even greater works."

After the re-introduction of spiritual healing many
mighty healing works were done. So much so, that great
edifices were erected in gratitude for marvelous healings
and works of reformation. Today we hear that healing
work does not compare to the early days in the field of
metaphysics, and yet we know that healings were not
accomplished by person, but by principle; not by
people, but by that mind which was in Christ Jesus. Is it
not clear then that we need, more than anything else, to
recapture the consciousness of the presence of that
mind? Must we not more clearly realize that mind is
man's only mind, omnipresent and omnipotent?

In ever growing degree must we understand the
consciousness that healed in the desert with Moses, in
Galilee with the Master, in Asia and Europe with Paul,
and with all the great modern pioneers of spiritual
healing in the 19th and 20th centuries. And the first step
is that it is not conscious thought which heals. The
consciousness we call Christ "takes no thought." The
healing consciousness is a "peace, be still" to error of
any name or nature, yet it acts in silence, and is expressed in quietness and confidence and peace.

The mind that was in Christ Jesus does not deny or
refute error, nor does it enter argument or discussion. It
knows that no denial is necessary. It knows that God is
not a power which one uses to destroy an evil power or
presence, because it knows no evil power or presence
exists; and in the presence of that which appears as sin,
sickness, or death, it rests in the assurance of Christ as
the only presence and as infinite perfection. Christ

consciousness needs no mental or audible reminders of truth. Its presence is the "peace, be still."

The mind that was in Christ Jesus is not attained by intellectual processes or reading more statements of truth. As one learns to still the human senses, learns to listen for the "still, small voice," the divine mind is understood and its presence definitely felt. In this awareness, the reality underlying the human picture becomes apparent. This apprehension of reality constitutes the activity and denotes the presence of the mind that was in Christ Jesus.

~

Human sense does not present a pretty picture, and even were it to be patched up, improved, or changed, it would still not be a spiritual picture, nor possess reality. Is it not clear then that not only does the picture need to be eliminated from consciousness, but even the consciousness itself which presented the picture should be given up, dissolved, so that not a trace remains. When we have learned that we have no mind but God, we shall know that there are no such pictures as those presented by physical sense, and that there is no other mind to conceive them.

In seeking the solution to a human problem, we often believe that some truth can or should open up to us which would meet our need; destroy the error, so to speak, and overcome the discord. Nothing can be further from the truth. That which I am seeking, I am. As we have no mind but God, our mind must be the truth that "healeth all our diseases." This very mind or consciousness embodies *now* and forever whatever truth, remedy, activity, or agency is needed at the moment. The truth which meets our need is the truth that our mind or consciousness *is* the truth itself; else how could Jesus say, "I am the truth."

Do not try to handle error as anything, to correct person, or strive to overcome discord, but rather begin *now* to see that your mind or consciousness is the power that reveals infinite harmony as being ever-present. This is the consciousness which declares, "I am the way." In other words, my mind, or consciousness, is the power. My mind or consciousness is the life. It embodies every quality, activity, and element of life. "I am the truth." I am the wine of inspiration; my mind or consciousness *is* (embodies) all the truth and life and inspiration for every occasion. Since there is no power apart from God, and we have no mind but God, there is no power apart from the mind which is God.

We must *rest* in this truth and not try to run away from problems, but watch the unfoldment of events which reveal our rightful place and true status, knowing continually that our mind or consciousness *is* or embodies the truth–the all truth, all the truth–and that there is no other mind or power.

A belief that we *need* some truth tries to come in, or, "If I only understood enough truth with which to meet this claim." Whereas, we must know that since the only mind we have is the mind called God that it itself, is the truth which makes us free. It (our individual mind, God) embodies *now* all the truth necessary.

Nothing can be added to the mind which is God, truth; indeed, nothing need be added. It is the truth itself which "healeth all thy diseases." We are not personal workers. We cannot work to remove or uncover error. Our work is to keep consciousness filled with all the truth we can imbibe and then let this consciousness of truth do the work.

The objectified universe is the *effect* of consciousness. Therefore, we cannot change or improve this universe in any way, but we can change our consciousness of the universe and then *let* this consciousness reveal the universe as it is. Our thought should not dwell on health or body or home, which to our imperfect sense may seem to need improving, but our thought should dwell on God, on the realization of the presence and power of a divine law operating in human consciousness to reveal the harmony of being. Our thought should dwell on the infinite nature of love, which cares for its creation through the laws of love and life. We should abide in the mind which expresses the eternal qualities of perfection. As our thought becomes imbued with this good, we, in turn, express this good in an improved form of body, of being, of health, of home.

A lecturer on his first trip to London arrived when the fog and mists were heaviest. Leaving the railroad station for the hotel, a sense of heaviness and fear overtook him (probably at what seemed such desolation). He wondered what was before him. Suddenly inspiration came and he realized that behind the mist was the city of London, a finished, perfect, complete city, in which each identity, each individual idea, was about "the Father's business," doing those things which were nearest at hand for him to do. This also brought the realization that behind his misty and foggy thought was his completed demonstration, his completed work, his receptive audiences. The fear lifted immediately. He saw that God created the world in *the beginning and saw that it was good,* whole, complete, harmonious, perfect. He saw every idea about "the Father's business," expressing perfection in the way of his appointing; the rose expressing beauty in its way and the lily expressing just as much beauty in another way; the musician expressing harmony and intelligence in his way and the artist expressing the same harmony and intelligence in another way. Each of us is expressing God in our individual way.

If I continue to look outside myself for the individualization of infinite power, I will be looking in the wrong direction. I individualize infinite power in proportion to my realization that there is but one mind, the divine mind, which is my mind. "I and the Father are one," means that if the Father is divine mind, my mind and that mind are one and the same mind. If the Father is divine life, then my life and the Father's life are the selfsame life.

$\sim$

"Let this mind be in you which was also in Christ Jesus."[4]

Because this mind is already your mind, you need "take no thought" for health, wealth, peace, or harmony. Rest in the truth that your mind is the truth, the life, the principle, and Soul of your being and body. Only by resting in this consciousness are we "letting" this mind of ours be all things to us.

It is natural that we should be tempted to think something, to "know the truth" about something, to make affirmations and denials, because these were the first steps we took when we were born into the new world of spirit. And these processes had their place then, and did good work for us then. But not now. The call has come to rise higher in understanding, to receive the meat of truth.

When we realize that "God is individual Mind,"[5] we understand that God is the mind of the individual and therefore, "the mind of the individual only can produce a result upon his body."[6] Is it not clear then that your mind is capable of governing you completely without the aid of words, formulas, prayers, or treatments?

Whatever form of error we have ever experienced is due only to the belief that we have a mind or life separate from God. The correction of this belief with the realization that God is our very mind, enables us to rest, to feel the peace that passeth understanding, and then harmony appears as naturally as light appears with the rising sun.

The belief that our mind is other than God has resulted in prayers to some other mind, in "communing" or "contacting" a divine mind. Truth reveals that this divine mind is your mind, the one mind, the only mind, the universal mind, which is the mind of the individual.

To rest in the consciousness of this truth is highest prayer. To know that God is the mind of the individual is to include the universe in your prayer.

~ 10 ~

THE REALM OF SOUL

There are no "small matters" in life. Harmony is the natural law of our being, and when there appears to be an absence of this in mind, body, or purse, it becomes a matter of importance. But here we are dealing with something different. It is not merely a matter of exchanging an inharmonious human condition for one of harmony. Something more is involved than a change of human conditions or feelings.

Human existence, as a rule, is just a round of changing outer experiences–some good and some bad. There are countless human methods of meeting these, from medical doctors to soul doctors.

To us, something entirely different enters the picture. Your experience has shown you that there is a world beyond this one, and yet a world here and now, possible of immediate attainment. This is the world you are seeking. The peace, harmony and perfection of that universe is beyond human understanding. The things of "this world" never touch that realm. When we have done as you have done, that is, risen above material sense into the kingdom of the mind, there remains this next step: the realm of Soul. Your work and your life now are mainly in the mental kingdom, but you must now reach for, or attain, the spiritual empire or realm of Soul.

Like the kingdom of mind, the spiritual empire is within you, but it is a higher level of consciousness–no doubt, the highest one.

No problem can be met on the level of the problem. So leave the problem behind you by rising to a new and higher state of consciousness. Jesus said, "My kingdom is not of this world."[1] Then, is it not necessary that we enter his "kingdom"? His "kingdom" is clearly not a mental one, because he taught that we are to "take no thought"; that taking thought will not add anything to us nor lead us into life and its harmonies. His "kingdom" is the realm of Soul, of inspiration and communion, a constant receptivity to good.

The Hebrew lad, Samuel, understood this vision and revealed it in his attitude of "Speak, Lord, thy servant heareth."[2] As also did Elisha where it is recorded, "And Elisha prayed, and said, Lord, I pray thee, open his eyes, that he may see. And the Lord opened the eyes of the young man; and he saw: and, behold, the mountain was full of horses and chariots of fire round about Elisha."[3] Nobody went anywhere; nobody changed anything; nobody prayed *for* anything. Just, the eyes are opened and we behold what already exists on the higher level of consciousness.

It is impossible for the human mind to conceive all the good there is for us, or even how to make it visible and tangible. It is only when we cease our human thinking, planning, outlining, affirming, and denying, and learn to *rest;* to "feel" God, to listen, that we are able to live by grace. Then our eyes being open, we are able to see the entire spiritual scene available here and now.

~

The attempt to understand truth through some relation to the world of form, results in a density of comprehension barring the reality from view. Only as we transcend the consciousness of finite form, do we catch glimpses of our divine being and of the spiritual universe in which we live and move.

There is no more resemblance between the real world and the scene we behold with the human eye, than there is between musical harmony and discord, or truth and error. Even the highest concept one can gain of the physical universe gives no hint of the beauty and magnitude of the incorporeal earth, in which is found no structural formation.

Spiritual sense, which is a consciousness completely freed of mortal concepts, alone beholds and reveals to individuals the world of truth, the earth of God's creating. All attempts to realize truth through the activity of the human mind must fail. We have been in spiritual darkness for many generations because of the incessant search for truth, carried on mainly in the realm of human knowledge. Truth is an impartation from the universal mind or consciousness within the individual. It is grasped in proportion to our ability to be receptive to the unfolding and revelation of truth within us, rather than on our ability to perceive it through mental striving. Not what we think or know, but what God reveals in us—this is the great secret. And the preparation for this holy experience is the patient waiting on God, the humble conviction that this is the Way.

Heaven cannot be taken by storm, or by striving, or by mental power. Heaven comes to the gentle stillness of the expectant thought. Heaven is the earth itself seen through the vision of the Soul. Earth is heaven itself seen through material sense.

"But there is a spirit in man: and the inspiration of the Almighty giveth them understanding."[4] Too often we accept some person of the past or present as authority, rather than seek the wisdom and inspiration of God. Yet, each of us has access to the same spirit for, as we learn here, "there is a spirit in man"–in all men.

Bronson Alcott writes: "The true teacher defends his pupils against his own personal influence. He inspires self-distrust. He guides their eyes from himself to the spirit that quickens him. He will have no disciple."

Is this not a clear direction for us to look beyond the person to the principle? It was Paul who said, ". . . and worshipped and served the creature more than the creator."[5] Let us always realize the infinity of our own being and draw therefrom our good. Our Soul is the infinite storehouse from which we draw our good. Emerson writes that "the powers of the Soul are commensurate with its needs, all experience to the contrary notwithstanding."

We have quoted from the Book of Job, from Romans, Bronson Alcott, and Emerson. Are these things true because these great lights uttered them? No. Let us ever remember that over the centuries great truths have been revealed by those close to God in consciousness– because these things were already true.

When we turn to inspired men, women, and books, let us always see behind the messenger to the message. Then we will find authority within ourselves, and confirmation and conviction whenever truth presents itself to us through person or book.

We never really love truth until some measure of it has come to us through our own consciousness. Then, we become fellows, friends, companions with all who have ever lived the same experience; we enter the very experiences of Jesus, Paul, John, and we share the thrills of all God-conscious men and women of all time. It makes us a part of the universal desire to bring the entire world into the awareness of the oneness of being. Our hearts throb with the hopes and dreams of the great revelators, and we know the same compassion they knew for the world that will not hear. It is a glorious company to join—the Soul-inspired of all ages. It is a possibility to you and to me as we seek, a little more each day, the empire of our own Soul.

~

We can only tune in to the universal mind or God-consciousness, through the mind that was in Christ Jesus, the intuitive sense. Never can the so-called human mind, the thinking mind, be an inlet to or an outlet from Christ-consciousness or the God mind. Spiritual sense is the avenue through which divine guidance, wisdom, and support come to us. Through spiritual sense alone we glimpse reality—the perfect universe behind the appearance or so-called material world.

This accounts for the fact that regardless of how much truth is known, declared or affirmed by the human mind, so little result in the way of healing is achieved. We are so eager for "results," so anxious to bring about healing, that we do not "wait on God." That is, we do not wait for mind to reveal the answer or perfection of being within us. We rush into "statements" and "truths" through the intellect; we affirm, deny and quote—all statements of truth, of course, but still not *truth* declaring itself; still not *mind affirming its own state of harmonious being.*

Let us never forget so-called healing is accomplished by spiritual sense, not by "taking thought," not by human reasoning, nor by repeating statements, nor by much quoting. You have no doubt heard it said over and over that, "I keep knowing the truth," or "I hold good thoughts," or "I read and read truth," (or other words to the same effect) "and yet do not heal or get healed." You may be assured that the "knowing" is actually being done *by* the person instead of *to* him or *within* him.

Yet, here lies the secret of success: "Wait on God." Be patient. We do not necessarily sit around in a chair with eyes closed, waiting. We go about our business; we perform all necessary duties; we study or do whatever lies at hand for us to do, and *let* the answer come in its own time. We go to sleep, if it's time for sleep, or take a walk or go to a show, and if nothing else presents itself, we may read an interesting book. *But keep thought off the problem. Let* the answer appear to us, within us. *Let* mind declare the perfection of its being and the nothingness of any other appearance. "Not by might, nor by power, but by my spirit."[6]

~ 11 ~

CONSCIOUSNESS

All that exists in the objectified realm is the creation or emanation of consciousness. Consciousness is the basic substance from which all manifestation issues forth. All that is, is the expression or formation of consciousness. It is consciousness that is the creative and governing principle of all forms and expressions, whether animate or inanimate, and which maintains and sustains its creation now and forever.

We must learn to view life from this standpoint, and then we will not too highly value anything in the manifested or objectified universe, knowing as we do, that the power of manifestation and jurisdiction is not in the objectified realm, but in the consciousness which has objectified itself as the universe. "Destroy this temple, and in three days I (consciousness) will raise it up."[1]

As there can be but one intelligence, one consciousness, it is your consciousness which is continually creating and re-creating your world, your experiences, your activity, your supply, and your environment. Your consciousness is the principle of your universe, and your universe is harmonious and successful in proportion to your realization of this truth.

Conscious thought is not God, is not creator. Conscious thought is but the tool with which consciousness operates. "Which of you by taking thought can add one cubit unto his stature?"[2] Taking thought is not the way of consciousness. Affirmations and denials are in the realm of human thought and do not express Deity. Consciousness alone is God. However, it is made known to human sense through thought, but thought itself is not the actor. It is the activity through which we become aware of the action and its effects, which is creation.

We must realize that our existence is the continuous and harmonious expression of spirit only in the degree that we learn to "be still," learn to "take no thought for your life, what ye shall eat; neither for the body, what ye shall put on." We must "consider the lilies" and note that "they toil not, they spin not; and yet . . . Solomon in all his glory was not arrayed like one of these."[3]

Your consciousness is the "all-in-all" to you. It creates, governs, protects, and perpetuates your entire universe, including your body. But you enjoy the continuity and harmony of being only in proportion to your ability to "take no thought"; to abide in the assurance of this truth; to let consciousness operate without interference of human belief, care, worry, or so-called assistance from "right thinking."

If you were in the midst of want, woe, or war, this consciousness would so direct your path that, "There shall no evil befall thee, neither shall any plague come nigh thy dwelling."[4] You would go through these experiences as Jesus went through walls, as the Hebrews went through the Red Sea and through the flames. When confronted by erroneous conditions of any nature, it is necessary to still your thought. "Peace, be still" is the solution for every care, for when human thought is stilled, pure consciousness is evident as the calm upon the waters.

It has been believed that digestion was in the digestive organs, elimination in the eliminative organs, strength in the muscles, life in the heart, etc. We should know and understand that all these are the activities of consciousness expressed by the body. We cannot, physically or mentally, correct erroneous conditions of body by seeking to correct the seemingly affected organs. We must realize and understand that as consciousness is the constructor of the body, so consciousness governs, protects, and perpetuates the body. That which appears as body or organs of the body is but the human concept of consciousness, of its formations. Our concept of body reflects our understanding of consciousness and of its operations and manifestation.

When the usual human sources and channels of supply, business, income, etc., become disrupted, it is necessary to realize and understand that your consciousness is the creative principle of your existence, and you must learn to rely on it to open new avenues of activity and income for you—with or without material accompaniment.

Become conscious of your true identity as consciousness, and you will see the world in its right relationship to yourself.

~

In belief, there is a state of consciousness called material, in which we apply a plaster to a pain in the back and a pill for a headache. Also, there is the belief of a mental state of consciousness, and in this mental state we find that our remedies consist of thoughts, mental formulas, or so-called prayers or treatments.

In the material realm theft is punished by prison, adultery by divorce or disease, and fear is manifested as disease or inflammation. In one case we are punished for physical violations, in the other we are victimized even for thinking sinful thoughts. In both cases we have cause and effect.

There is no criticism for either of these states of consciousness. In human experience we progress from one level of thought to another. Moses gave us the law, but Jesus raised us into the mental realm, and those who could follow him into the highest realm, he raised to spiritual consciousness.

"The human self must be evangelized"[5] and "purification of sense and self"[6] is necessary. We should continually strive to overcome in ourselves the negative qualities of impatience, impurity, condemnation, judging, criticizing, moralizing, fault-finding, doubting, fearing. We cannot put into vessels already full of these qualities the "new wine" of inspiration wherewith we rise above both the physical and mental into spiritual consciousness, where there is "nothing that defileth or maketh a lie"–nothing to be denied, overcome, eliminated, or destroyed.

In this state of consciousness error never presents itself to us as either person, place, or thing. We do not have to deny anything nor search for some truth to apply as a remedy. There, we "stand still and see the salvation of the Lord." We close our eyes and turn from person or situation and "feel" the presence of God; or realize the love of God; or become conscious of God's law wisely and lovingly governing all of his creation.

This is the "sensing" or "feeling" or "awareness" of good. We feel love for all of God's creation, we reach the Christ-man. In this consciousness there is nothing to meet, heal, or be healed. There is no need for a ten or thirty minute treatment. What we need is a spiritual state of consciousness, which is developed by practice. "Blessed are they which do hunger and thirst after righteousness: for *they shall be filled*"[7] with the "conscious, constant capacity to understand God"[8] through "prayer, without ceasing."

This is dwelling every moment in the consciousness of love, joy, peace, harmony, and letting error go without giving it too much thought; without fear or concern, because without thought, fear, or concern error will vanish of its own nothingness. Human thought is the substance of disease and disaster. Therefore, when thought is withdrawn from a problem, it has no substance to support or sustain it. "Which of you by taking thought can add one cubit unto his stature?"[9] Take thought off the so-called problem and the problem must go, because its only substance is the human thought of which it is formed. It may be either conscious or unconscious thought that causes and continues the appearance of discord.

Everything exists in the universal consciousness, or divine mind. Sun, moon, stars, animals, and plants, all have their being as individual idea in mind, as forms of consciousness, as formations of spirit, as expressions of life, and all live and move in accord with the infinite law of divine principle. This principle is impartial and absolute, and governs impartially all of its creation.

Divine mind, universal consciousness, is, therefore, forever conscious of its ideas, and conscious also of the harmonious relationship existing between all these ideas, as a natural result of the reign of principle.

All students of metaphysics will readily agree on these fundamental truths, but we need to be sure of the next step. We must recognize that this universal consciousness is our own individual consciousness, for there is but one.

Every quality of divine love, every faculty of infinite mind, every law of principle, every activity of eternal life, which is embraced in divine consciousness is individually expressed *as* you and me. This should be carefully studied, because it underlies an understanding that every student of truth must recognize and accept if he is to do the "greater works."

We are never dependent on any condition, circumstance, or person, but have always within our own consciousness the "fulness of the Godhead bodily." *All* that comprises the universal consciousness is manifested as individual consciousness.

Every quality of life, infinity, and eternality, is expressed in your individual life. Every faculty of divine mind is *perfectly* expressed in each individual. The peace, harmony, power, health, and wealth of the Father is forever maintained in the life and being of every son and daughter of love, through the Christ in individual consciousness.

In reality, in seeking truth you reached out for the Christ. You therefore left behind that which you call your personal consciousness so that you might rise to the universal consciousness, the Christ-consciousness. In this divine consciousness, there is freedom from personality and the limitations of the past, present, or future. Here, we find no limited or limiting sense of faculties, of opportunities, of anything pertaining to life, joy and power.

The qualities of finiteness which seemed to bind you before you reached the recognition of the Christ in

human consciousness, drop away in your newer consciousness; in your awareness of the infinity of being—the
infinite nature of *your* being.

In mind, infinite consciousness, there are "many
mansions"—many states of consciousness—and all good
and all eternal. When you left your state of personal
selfhood to enter the Christ-consciousness, you accepted
for yourself the "Mind that was in Christ Jesus." In this
mind, your consciousness, you found your perfect vision
(spiritual discernment)—the recognition of the Christ in
human consciousness.

The Christ-mind is active in you as your consciousness, as your awareness, as your vision and hearing, as
your understanding. These faculties belong to mind, and
are the activities of your mind expressed "unto eternity."

Entering this Christ-consciousness, under the dominion of the Christ-mind, you leave behind the beliefs of
personal sense, the false activities of a so-called human
selfhood, and you enter the joys of true being, of infinite
life and mind, where you express the larger, fuller
concept of being, and where you reflect the infinitude of
the changeless divine consciousness. No longer are you
dependent on a finite concept of yourself, but yours is
now the "wide horizon," the "larger, broader, grander
view." No longer is your vision confined to the experience, environment, or inheritance of the personal sense
of being, but you are "heirs of God, and joint-heirs with
Christ"—heirs to the infinitude of the Christ-mind and
the Christ-life.

The only substance of being is the infinite, universal
consciousness, free from all so-called laws or beliefs in
matter or material conditions. Life is the shining forth of
this consciousness, in which is included every element of

harmony, peace, joy, activity, abundance, and health. (The latter only as perfection, with no sense of discord, decomposition or death.) In life there is no fear or its consequent result, no power or presence to anything but the perpetual harmonious activity of conscious perfection.

In human existence distortions appear, taking the form of beliefs in opposition to actual understanding or reality. These false beliefs come to us as so-called natural laws, and their attendant suffering for violation of them. They are, however, *not laws,* but beliefs, and are made null and void by the understanding of the truth that no law of humanity, no law of human origin, no law of material creation *is law,* and, any and all of these are without power, cause, or effect. Nothing that seems materially true is true; nothing that is materially discerned is real; nothing that is claimed for matter has any basis. None of these have any place in the pure consciousness of life—which is man—and none have power for good or evil.

This may seem beautiful as abstract philosophy, but we may specifically apply this truth to any problem of human existence and find, not only that this is truth, but, further, that this truth protects and governs man. This is the God "who healeth all thy diseases," and this is the only law on which the harmony of health, home, and supply are maintained.

This life, which is pure consciousness, embraces no hint of disease, disaster, flood, or famine; it knows no accident or breakage, age or change, wealth or poverty; it recognizes no comparative good or evil, sinlessness or sinfulness, because it is conscious only of infinite and eternal perfection, in which there is no element of time, change, or belief. True consciousness, which is the life of all being, knows only the *allness of being;* the allness of infinite and eternal perfection, without change, and without effect from human opinions or actions. We are therefore never aware of sin or sickness: these are the shadows of a belief held in thought, but which are overcome with the truth of reality.

Recognize that your consciousness knows no matter, and you will appreciate the impossibility of age, change, decay, and discord; you will appreciate the vacuity of disease as the nothingness of a false belief. Thus, it will have no more power to pain, cause suffering, or discord than any shadow could.

It is a wrong concept in universal thought, consciously or unconsciously accepted, which is imaged forth (expressed) as an imperfection in or on the body, and it is necessary to supplant this wrong concept with the truth, or right concept, to bring about a healing. The mind will then express the light of understanding, instead of the false belief that formerly occupied it.

At this point we find ourselves individual consciousness, never in nor of matter; never in nor of the dream of material life or death; never conscious of material limitations or conditions, but continually aware of divine perfection, harmonious being, and completeness; forever experiencing freedom, unlimited life and health; forever expressing unbounded harmonious activity and the infinite capacity to know, to think, to live, to love, and to *be.*

Consciousness of the presence of the universal mind and its activities meets every problem of human existence. In this higher consciousness we cannot acknowledge that there is a patient. The patient, so-called, is neither person, place, nor thing, and all that can be designated as such exists in the manifested realm as effect only.

Applying a material remedy, let us say medicine, to an effect such as disease, is the application of one manifested thing to another. It is done under the illusion that a greater power (medicine) can overcome a lesser power (disease). Going higher into the mental realm, we find thoughts being applied to beliefs; as, for instance, a thought of health is applied to a belief of disease. Moses almost attained the supreme demonstration of understanding, but yet failed to reach the Promised Land (the height of understanding) because he saw God as a great power, supreme over lesser powers. Christ Jesus, however, attained the ultimate. He saw God as omnipotence, the all-power, the one and only power.

We apply neither material remedies nor mental thoughts. We recognize no lesser powers to be overcome or destroyed, but stand firmly in the Christ-consciousness—"He that seeth me, seeth Him that sent me."[10] Then, is it not clear that since there is but one universal mind, this same mind must be your mind and my mind? Also, since there is but one eternal life, it must be your life and my life.

This universal mind and eternal life is expressed as one infinite body, which incorporates within itself all the nature, character, qualities, and activities of mind and life. It is spiritual and indestructible, and is individually expressed in all its glory as your mind and my mind, as your life and my life, as your body and my body.

Would you treat this universal mind, which is your mind, or this eternal life which is your life? Could you treat this infinite body, which is your body? When we accept this truth that mind, life, body, individually expresses itself, its activities, its qualities, and the harmony of its being as you and as me, we have "put off the old man," (mortal consciousness) and we have put on the mind that was in Christ Jesus; we have attained the Christ-consciousness.

In this pure consciousness of love, erroneous beliefs and conditions disappear from our human experience as naturally as darkness vanishes from the presence of light and yet, even more than this, we impersonally heal all those who come within range of our consciousness without conscious effort, in the same way that the woman was healed by touching the hem of Christ's robe.

Each time one becomes conscious of the presence of God some phase of personal selfhood disappears. To "pray without ceasing" is to be continually conscious of the presence of God. How may this be done in the hustle and bustle of everyday life? The student of truth will gradually prepare himself for the unfoldment of this state of consciousness by learning to look away from all manifested form or thought when confronted with any situation that needs correction. As long as thought is on the level of manifestation, we are not in the "secret place of the most High," where infinite perfection is eternally expressed. As long as thought is on the person or condition, we are seeing a selfhood apart from God, and there is no basis for our understanding. We should never acknowledge person, place, or thing, but in all cases immediately lift thought to mind and its harmonious ideas, to life and its eternal expression, to love and its comforting presence, to spirit and its indestructible substance, to principle and its changeless law.

The consciousness that knows this truth realizes that universal mind impersonally expresses its intelligence, sanity, and guidance as all men; that eternal life is manifested as all being, (and eternal life could not, if it would, withdraw itself from *any* manifestation); that divine love impartially protects and sustains all its children; that indestructible spirit is supporting its every formation; and that infinite principle is maintaining the infinity and eternality of all creation through its divine law of good.

In this consciousness there is no one to heal or to be healed; no person to harm or to be harmed; no evil condition to overcome; no belief or power to touch the divine consciousness, nor any of its infinite individualized creation. The consciousness of the presence of God dispels the illusion of any other presence. The consciousness of the presence of universal mind dispels the fear of any person or circumstance. The consciousness of the presence of infinite principle eliminates the belief in any material or mental law. This is Christ-consciousness, and it automatically blesses, protects, saves, and heals all those who come within its sphere.

Life, viewed from the standpoint of divine consciousness, shows us that God is infinite good, eternal life, the source of all activity; that God is principle, the law of the harmonious government of the universe, including man. He is the creator of all that is, and maintains this universe by means of tender love and supreme wisdom.

We are a state of consciousness in which infinite good, eternal life and harmonious activity is forever maintained. We are pure. We are infinite good manifested as individual consciousness. We are the embodiment of the ideas of pure mind, and we are tributary to Soul, through which the perfect qualities of eternal life are forever expressed.

It may readily be seen from this that illusion, whether physical or mental, has no reality and can never be incorporated in God's creation. The mind of man, which is God, ever expresses itself as pure thoughts, spiritual ideas. This mind is omniscience and contains not a single element of discord. This mind, the consciousness of the individual, is conscious only of the perfection of infinite being, universally and individually expressed.

These statements of truth may be demonstrated by all seekers of truth, in the degree that these laws are accepted, understood, and applied.

Frequently students are found who have worked unsuccessfully for long periods to overcome some phase of physical, mental, or financial discord. Should these faithful ones but realize that the claim, regardless of the name or nature, is not theirs, is not their own belief or thought, but that the false belief, thought, or claim, is but a part of the vast mental illusion which is forever without mind to express it, and without law to enforce it, then even the most malicious or chronic condition will yield. "The peace that passeth understanding" comes with the realization that evil does not exist even as a claim or belief.

When we come to the point of recognizing that the claim is not a part of our individual consciousness; that the belief is not our belief, in fact, that it is a belief without a believer, then we are on the high road to freedom from the erroneous manifestation.

Truth interprets and exemplifies the Biblical teaching regarding spirituality, and immortality. John says, "Beloved, now are we the sons of God,"[11] and Paul states that we are "heirs of God, and joint-heirs with Christ."[12] We are the infinite capacity to receive and respond to truth, love, health, and wealth; to know eternal life, harmony, and wholeness of immortal being. Individual spiritual consciousness contains not one element of error, discord, disease, inharmony, or lack, but is substance, spirit, and reality.

Incorporeal, composed of the substance of spirit, and containing not one iota of matter or material belief, we are spirit, infinite mind, and eternal life made manifest—"the Word made flesh."

When we are no longer limited by the five physical senses and have attained even a measure of spiritual sense, or Christ-consciousness, we find ourselves unlimited in terms of "here" or "there," "now" or "hereafter." There is a going in and coming out without sense of time or space; an unfolding without degree; a realization without an object.

In this consciousness finite sense disappears and the vision is without boundaries. Life is seen and understood as unfettered form and limitless beauty. Even the wisdom of the ages is encompassed in a moment. Death disappears and once more we see those previously separated from us by this so-called impassable barrier. This communion is not the communication of spiritualism, but an awareness of eternal life untouched by death. It is the reality of immortality seen and understood. It is a vision of life without beginning and with no end. It is reality brought to light.

In this consciousness there are no physical barriers of time and space. The vision encompasses the universe. It bridges time and eternity. It includes all being.

In this light we see without the eye; we hear without the ear; we understand things not known before. Where we are, God is, because there is no longer separation or division. Here there are no rewards and no punishment. Harmony is. Life is not dependent on processes; we do not live by bread alone.

Spiritual sense is not engaged with human good and yet, this Christ-consciousness reveals the harmony of being in what appears as our human experience, and in forms available to our present circumstance. Though "my kingdom is not of this world," yet, "your Father knoweth that ye have need of these things" and he supplies your wants even before you ask. (See Luke 12:22-32.)

Study "Our Real Existence" in *The Infinite Way*.

～

The more I watch the practice and all the various forms of activity, the more convinced I become that spiritual sense alone is the answer to every problem. Not how many statements of truth we know; not from what angle we understand metaphysical writings, but our spiritual sense is healer, supplier, reformer; our spiritual sense of existence brings out the harmony of life.

Our work is not in the realm of persons, things, or conditions. Harmony becomes apparent in our lives in proportion as we stop working on or for persons and things and spiritualize our sense of consciousness; spiritualize our sense of life, its formations and activities. Jesus' statement: "My kingdom is not of this world"[13] has tremendous significance, because, was he not here on earth partaking of the things of this world, teaching the people of this world? To me this means that we are free, harmonious, only as we cease taking thought for the things of "this world" and *let* the divine harmonies of reality appear and lift us above our false concepts of this world, to "the apprehension of divine ideas."

Nevertheless, it is through consciousness that we realize happiness and contentment. We must not look to person or circumstance for these. They do not come from person or thing. Certainly before we come to an understanding of truth, we appear to get our joy from money, home, wife, husband, parent, children, but as we grow in understanding we find that these are only the channels through which good seems to come to us. Ultimately, however, we have to find our good within our own consciousness, independent of person or thing or place.

We must look to our *principle* for all our good. Then, if here or there a human fails us, or even if the whole human picture seems to fail us, our good will still be omnipresent in tangible form, though probably from an entirely different source than we anticipated.

It is from spiritual consciousness that we derive our good, our happiness, our contentment. The consciousness of the omnipresence of good within us is our anchor in spirit. "My kingdom is not of this world." Therefore, I do not have to look to it for my good, but to the center of my being.

Spiritual consciousness reverses the material senses in which good must flow *to* us, and reveals true spiritual joy, reveals good flowing out *from* the center of our being—where we do not seek good, or seek happiness or contentment. We seek only the opportunity to *let* good flow out from us.

This takes thought away from a human sense of selfhood, which seems always to be in need of some one or some thing, and enables us to demonstrate our divinity, or Christhood. "My kingdom is not of this world." Therefore, do not busy yourself making a better or healthier or happier human, but stay in the kingdom of reality, where there is neither person, place nor thing, and where harmony is the ever-present reality.

If we are successful in maintaining this position firmly, we will find everything in our experience expressing or manifesting the harmony, the activity, the abundance, the perfection of our perfect principle.

~ 12 ~

MIND AND ITS IDEA ONE

Mind and its idea, life and its expression, these are one, inseparable and indivisible. The continuity of life is maintained by infinite and eternal law, or principle. The Son of God is forever one with the Father. That which God has created is forever manifested. In other words, life cannot be deprived of its manifestation; spirit cannot lose its formations, mind cannot be separated from its ideas; love always expresses itself, and the varied expressions of love are eternal and immortal.

This is true of God and man, of God and his activity. God, life, truth, love, harmony, perfection, all these are infinite in being and in manifestation. Error, evil, disease are appearances without entity or identity, without presence or power, without law, action, volition, or continuity. Having no law to enforce them, they have no being; having no cause or creator, they do not exist as effect. Infinite life, its activity and harmony are eternally expressed as God's manifested being—man and the universe. There is not a single element of error, discord, or fear in either God or his son, in mind or its idea, in spirit or its formations, in life or its expressions. This is the law of life and the law of mind—the ever-operating law of good. It reveals the reality of being, dispelling the false appearances of sense. This is the law unto you.

The basic premise of Christian Science is that God is infinite being and that man is *that being expressed* in all its perfection and harmony. Therefore, a sick, sinning, evil, unkind, ungenerous man has no existence anywhere at any time, and the *belief that there is such a man must be overcome in your thought.* "Man is the expression of God's being"[1]–"God is infinite, therefore ever present, and there is no other power nor presence."[2] It follows, then, that *you* are being called upon to refute the testimony of the senses and to behold "in Science the perfect man . . . where sinning mortal man appears to mortals."[3] This statement applied to human affairs leads to the truth about God and man. If you do not do this, you are accepting yourself and others as less than divine being.

Make a definite effort every day to remember that you are the manifestation of God's being; that you are life, God, expressed; that you are the "Word made flesh;" that you are incorporeal, spiritual "and your life is hid with Christ in God;" "For in him we live, and move, and have our being;" that you are "in the secret place of the most High;" and that this is true of all men, regardless of any appearance to the contrary.

~

The time has come to get serious in this work of understanding and living truth. What have you in thought? Is it a desire to express more love, to be more humanly good, more helpful, more charitable; more patient, more tender, more forgiving? As necessary as these things are, they do not constitute love in a spiritual sense.

To love more means to know the relationship of God to his manifestation. What does "God and his manifestation" mean to you? Do you understand that God and his manifestation are one, that is, God manifested? Or do you believe there is God and manifestation also? God manifested is man. Therefore, man is purely the manifestation of the qualities and attributes of God. It naturally follows that man cannot have a single quality or trait that is not a constituted part of God, because God being "all-in-all" there is no other source from which any quality or attribute could be derived.

What of the unlovely traits we see in human conduct? From the basis of God as "all-in-all," there can be no such thing, and what seem to be these evils are merely illusions, forged by the belief that this is a material universe and that man is a material being, instead of a state of consciousness. In other words, all the seeming evils are the product of the finite physical senses like the illusions we see in the desert. The desert illusions have no actual substance, because all that is there to be seen is a combination of sun, air, and sand, and yet, all the while we are looking at these, a distorted imagination conjures up a full-grown village.

The illusions of sickness or poverty—discord in any form—have no more substance than the desert village. First, you indulge the belief that you are taking cold then a cough follows, then a fever, and the first thing you know we believe we have a full-grown illness, just as in the desert village we had water, trees, houses, people—all in belief. Why is this so? "A mortal belief fulfills its own conditions."[4]

This unmistakably shows that the false sense and all its evidence are one sheer illusion—because man, as God's manifestation, lacks nothing that he requires to be the full and complete representation of his divine principle. We must cease giving power to human efforts and abide securely in the power of spiritual consciousness. We are not affected by the things of the world, by external conditions, when we consciously live in spiritual consciousness—the consciousness of his presence and power. "Greater is he that is in you, than he that is in the world."[5] This statement gives us the assurance of the presence and power of the omnipresent and omnipotent Christ within us, ever ready and able to meet every situation; to reverse every seeming adverse circumstance, and to recognize the reign of good, the government of divine principle in our affairs. Harmony throughout the universe is the law of God, the principle of infinite good.

Immortality cannot be bestowed on a human being, any more than spiritual understanding can be conferred on anyone. The consciousness of this truth comes to individual thought in proportion to our ability to let go human considerations that bind to the belief of life in matter. After all, your consciousness embodies all the truth there is. It is the kingdom of God within you; not far off in some vague divine mind or spiritual consciousness, but in the divine mind or spiritual consciousness which is your mind and consciousness. This removes the mystery, the miracle, and dissolves the illusions.

⁓

How do we know when it is the Christ speaking? When we have received an impartation of intelligence, love, understanding, joy, freedom from the Christ, it is always followed with conviction and we are certain of its message. "I will listen for thy voice" and I will recognize it, for no other voice is like it; none other has its authority, its dignity, its certainty.

What is the relationship of God to man? On this point hinges the entire demonstration of spiritual understanding. *Oneness* is the relationship of God to man. The divine mind is the mind of man; the one infinite life is the life of man; the divine being is man's only being. Then, what else is there of man but God? Oneness brings out the right idea; it indicates one and no more: oneness of being, oneness of life, oneness of mind.

God cannot be explained to anyone, he must be realized. As far as it is possible to explain God and his relation to man and the universe, I would say that we must strive to get the consciousness that God is the mind of man, he is the life of man. In periods of communion still the human mind with short quieting statements like, "peace, be still"–"In quietness and confidence shall be my strength"–"My peace I give unto you"–"Be still and know that I am God." When you have achieved a sense of stillness, let the word God be present in your thought until revelation appears. Try it often until inspiration has brought the conscious awareness of God.

Impartations of truth come from within. They are the direct result of our understanding that, as man is mind manifested, he is and must ever be the harmonious God-being, and any appearance to the contrary cannot change the fact. "Treat a belief in sickness as you would sin, with sudden dismissal."[6] However, you can do this only when you have reached the assurance that man *is* spiritual, perfect, and needs no healing.

In proportion as you live in the calm assurance of God as the only presence and power can you release yourself from mental argument. As conviction comes to you of man's relationship to God as God manifested, as life expressed, can you realize the harmony of being which knows no fear of sin or disease. Uppermost in thought must be the understanding that even that which appears to ignorant, illusive sense as error, is suggestion;

that which is called accident, under action or overaction, is mirage or nothingness.

Then, we do not attempt to heal, correct, improve, but we rest—yes, we rest in the certainty that "as in heaven, so on earth, God is omnipotent, supreme."[7] Silence human thinking by learning to listen; by stilling the material senses with, "peace, be still."

~

Progress is divine perfection unfolding in consciousness, and this perfection unfolds in consciousness in proportion to one's ability and willingness to receive, acknowledge, and respond to it. This perfection, being omnipresent, is ever awaiting your recognition and acceptance, and this recognition and acceptance leads us to an important revelation.

What is this omnipotent and omnipresent divine perfection? It is known by many names. It has been called the real man, the spiritual self, the presence, divine spirit, the Father within, the presence of God, spirit of God, the Christ, and no doubt many others beside. Actually, it is you. It is the reality of your being, the I AM THAT I AM, the "only "I", of us," the infinite eternal you, which, when recognized and accepted, governs, controls, and heals that which we know as the human concept, your so-called human selfhood.

At first glance this sets up two men, but let us not be fooled, because this presence, Christ, or Father within, is you; the only reality of your being. The so-called human selfhood is merely the mortal concept of that divine you, and as long as you eat, sleep, and bathe, there will seem to be this you. Some saw this concept in Jesus as the son of a carpenter, or of Mary, while Peter (enlightened consciousness) recognized it as "the Christ, the Son of the living God."

Several times a day stop whatever you are doing and admit this Christ, or divine presence, into your conscious awareness; recognize its presence, its power and dominion. Acknowledge it as your true identity, your savior, your real being. Accept it as the presence that goes before you to "make the crooked places straight, "as your ever-present guard, guide, comforter, supporter, and supplier; yea, more, your comfort and supply.

"Behold, I stand at the door, and knock"[8] and this "I" is the Christ, your real selfhood, the divinity of your being. For this reason, we do not pray, petition, plead, or even try to deserve good in any form, because the good which we seek is the very reality of us, and we must open consciousness to the recognition of this truth.

This "I", or Christ, or Father within, is your consciousness, the one and only being, and, therefore, it is the consciousness of all men. The recognition of this one and only consciousness as yours and mine, and the acceptance of the divinity of being, is fulfilling your duty "to love thy neighbor as thyself." "If a man say, I love God, and hateth his brother, he is a liar: for he that loveth not his brother whom he hath seen, how can he love God whom he hath not seen?"[9] Of course, God is the consciousness of man and in loving (recognizing and acknowledging) the divinity of man, you are loving God.

The Christ of you, the divine spirit within does not ask for favors or wait for time or circumstances. Realize it as the divinity, or reality, of your being, ever with you, and from the moment of this recognition you will see your life change. The infinite power of good comes into conscious awareness, bringing with it the forces of healing, activity, success, supply, good in all forms.

Silence the action of the brain and personal will, and let your consciousness be flooded with the reality of your being, your true selfhood, the Christ or Son of God, which you are.

~ 13 ~

SPIRITUAL HEALING

Spiritual healing is a delicate subject, easily misunderstood by those not having had much experience in healing without mental argument. Therefore, it is necessary that it be rightly presented.

It is possible for everyone to learn that spiritual consciousness does the work. And spiritual consciousness is cultivated through study, communion, and practice. It is the result of living every moment in the conscious awareness of good as all, and through the recognition that there is no error.

Spiritual healing shows that the impartation is always from mind to its idea, and this constitutes the Word of God, which is "quick, and powerful, and sharper than any two-edged sword"; also, that the thoughts of man, the human thoughts, mental arguments, do not constitute that Word. Two things are important here: receptivity and reflection.

As we become receptive to divine mind, through the stilling of the senses, divine impartations do come to us. Sometimes they are in thought original to ourselves, or, as the case may be, quotations from the Bible or other writings. Then, again there may be just a "feeling" or a sense of uplifted consciousness; a sense or awareness of rightness.

When these divine ideas come to us, we reflect on them; we see them in their relation to the immediate problem. Mental argument is of itself not a healer, but it may serve to uplift thought to a point receptive to the right idea. Also, when argument is used (affirmations and denials), one should not consider the work complete, but "be still" and await the answer which never fails to come. Thus, the treatment is not the declaration, but the period after the declaration, when one is listening to "the still, small voice." The awareness, or consciousness of good that follows is the healer, the Christ, spiritual consciousness.

It is important at some time in one's experience that we learn the part gratitude plays in having the correct sense of substance; to ascertain within ourselves if we know the truth about supply and gratitude. So long as we believe that supply and gratitude are things a person can either give or withhold, we are faced with the necessity of correcting this false belief.

Supply and gratitude are qualities, or attributes of divine mind. Therefore, they are ever-present in individual consciousness. We cannot receive supply or gratitude for these are omnipresent ideas of mind, embodied in man and continually expressed in individual consciousness. Any belief to the contrary must be corrected.

We cannot look to person, place, thing, circumstance, or condition for supply or gratitude. We must realize their omnipresence as ideas. "Man has no Mind but God."[1] With complete reliance on this truth, we look *only* to the one mind, the mind of individual man, and there find *all* good.

～

Just a few lines on healing. What accomplishes the healing? *Science and Health* has revealed that it is in the answer to the question, "Whom do men say that I the

Son of man am?"[2] This "I" heals. It is the Christ, the "Father in heaven," the principle of life, the principle of man. It is not man, nor medicine, nor creed, nor rites, nor worship, which heals, but "I" the impersonal presence. It needs no human help from either matter or human thought. Truth reveals "I" as the Christ, and that Christ is God—the life and Soul of man. Also, that neither creed nor prayer make a Christian.

Man has not a mind separate from deity. Disease is merely belief, which will be healed immediately by destroying the belief. Where is this belief? Is it in the mind of your patient? Never. The belief is that of general human consciousness, collectively, and must be destroyed there. As a general rule, you may forget your patient as soon as he has unburdened himself to you, since the belief is not his own. It is the belief of collective human consciousness using the individual as a channel to express the belief.

Be careful not to accept the belief as either your own or your patient's. Nullify it where you find it, in general or collective human consciousness. Know, also, that human consciousness is illumined because there is but one consciousness and this one divine; that mortal consciousness has no substance, no law, no continuity, no cause, and can have no effect, no channel for its transmission or expression; then, you are on your way to victory.

The belief is never more than appearance having no reality; a mirage with no power, no presence, no activity. There is no mind to create, to perpetuate, to receive or to respond to such conditions. In other words, there is no mind to manifest as this appearance or belief, because there is but one mind, your mind, which

intelligence, love, outpouring, wholeness

manifests and expresses infinite intelligence, perfect understanding, and harmony eternally.

To sum it all, error must be seen as appearance only, without form or being; the product of non-existing mortal mind or consciousness. That right where this appearance seems to be, there is perfect mind manifested; life unfolded; spirit imaged forth; love reflected. Finally, that there is but one mind, one life, one intelligence, and this *one* infinitely, eternally, and harmoniously expressed. *One without a second. Not two. There is none beside me (God)."*

As there are no spiritual organs to function, all must be the activity of consciousness. So-called material organs or functions are human symbols which counterfeit the activities of mind. Above all, lose the sense of having a patient. If there is but one mind, there can be but one manifestation.

~

Freedom from fear comes only with the recognition that the divine "I" is our only selfhood. We know that the divine "I" is God, and therefore I AM that which is invisible to mortal sense, and that which is "hid with Christ in God." This "I" is self-possessed, self-maintained, self-sufficient, and complete. It contains within itself all life, all love, all being, and these as forever harmoniously expressed.

The "I" that I AM is the "Father within," and is "greater . . . than he that is in the world," that is, greater than any circumstance or condition. Recognizing this "I" to be the directing source of infinite good, we learn to depend more and more on the presence and the power within "to prepare a place" for us, "to make the crooked places straight," and to make the desert blossom as the rose. Never more shall we look outside the divine Self, the I AM. After all attention has been withdrawn from the manifested realm and placed on the "I" that I AM, then will we see God, good, even though we are yet in the flesh.

When a healthy man directs his feet to carry him in one direction, he does not find himself walking in the opposite direction. He knows that this is because "he" has dominion over his feet. He also knows that his body is not he, but the visible manifestation of him; the vehicle or form through which he expresses and moves himself. Is it not clear, then, that he, the man, is invisible, incorporeal and free from any so-called mental or physical conditions? This *he,* which seems to be a very personal and separate being, is the impersonal, universal I AM, individually expressing itself as you and as me.

Consciousness of the truth that this "I" that I AM is God, is liberating, because it enables us to perceive that I AM not in bondage to physical organs or functions; that I AM not subject to rents, bills, and debts; but that I AM spiritually clothed, fed, housed, and therefore I AM without problems of health, home, intelligence, or wealth.

Do you recall the astonishment of Moses when he realized, "I AM THAT I AM"[3]? It was through this understanding that Isaiah could say, "My word . . . shall not return unto me void, but it . . . shall accomplish that which I please, and it shall prosper in the thing whereto I sent it."[4] Turning to Christ Jesus, we find these startling words: "He that seeth me seeth him that sent me,"[5] and "the words that I speak unto you, they are spirit, and they are life."[6]

At first glance many may believe that these inspired teachings refer only to the great men who uttered them.

Many believe that these, and other great leaders of religious thought, have been divinely inspired, so that their words have greater weight or mightier power than others, but these words of Christ Jesus correct the fallacy: "Verily, verily, I say unto you, He that believeth on me, the works that I do shall he do also; and greater works than these shall he do; because I go unto my Father."[7]

In order to know that there is but one universal "I", and that every individual is the individualized expression of that I THAT I AM, we can look to the words of the Bible and find that which concerns you and me—the "Son of Man."

Daniel declares: "I saw in the night visions, and, behold, one like the Son of man came with the clouds of heaven, and came to the Ancient of days, and they brought him near before him. And there was given him dominion, and glory, and a kingdom, that all people, nations, and languages, should serve him: his dominion is an everlasting dominion, which shall not pass away, and his kingdom that which shall not be destroyed. And the kingdom and dominion, and the greatness of the kingdom under the whole heaven, shall be given to the people of the saints of the most High, whose kingdom is an everlasting kingdom, and all dominions shall serve and obey him."[8]

"Shall obey" whom? The Son of man, who also is "the people of the most High," the "Son of God." That you and I may know that the "Son of man" is one with the "Son of God," and is empowered with all the dominion of the I AM, Christ Jesus gave us the eternal message of man's divinity: "But that ye may know that the Son of man hath power on earth to forgive sins, (then saith he to the sick of the palsy,) Arise, take up thy bed, and go unto thine house,"[9] and, also, that we might know that this particular "Son of man" is not set apart with special power. We may remind ourselves that he said, "greater works" shall we do.

In the sixth chapter of Luke we find Jesus relating the story of David eating the shewbread, which was held for priests alone; this in defense of his disciples for plucking the corn on the Sabbath. He said, "The Son of man is Lord also of the Sabbath."[10]

Ever and ever the question arises: "Who is this Son of man?" And again and again the Christ reveals: "Yet a little while is the light with you. Walk while ye have the light, lest darkness come upon you: for he that walketh in darkness knoweth not whither he goeth."[11] And God said unto Ezekiel, "Son of man, stand upon thy feet, and I will speak unto thee."[12] To every one who listens for the voice of God, for the revelation of the spiritual consciousness, comes the "still, small voice," breathing the sacred answer to the Master's question: "Whom do men say that I the Son of man am?"–"Thou art the Christ, the Son of the living God."[13]

～

We must have the courage to leave the old landmarks of theology, mentology, and the beaten path of others, for an original or, rather, individual mode of expression as God shows one in meditation, prayer, and silence.

The secret of secrets is this: never try to heal matter as matter. This is the password to success in practice and demonstration. Never try to remove or reduce a growth, increase or decrease blood pressure, heal a burn, reduce a fever, overcome a cold, etc. We are not physicians and we have nothing to do with healing bodies. We have, by the grace of good, been given the revelation that this is a spiritual universe, that we are entirely spiritual, that we have perfect, spiritual bodies, and that *our work* is to correct the belief that man, including the universe, is material and mortal. We do not treat a person or a body. Our work is impersonal. It is treating the world belief in any given direction. That is why we cannot look to the body for health, or to see if we are improving.

Once you agree, through understanding, that there is a principle governing and controlling its universe, you can never again believe there is disease or sin or war; and any picture before the senses *must* be understood to be illusion. An illusion can never be objectified, can it? This understanding brings with it a peace, a surety, a poise, a power, against which no belief can prevail. So, then, we never need to fight error, sin, or discord. Just quietly, lovingly, and above all peacefully, speak the Word of truth, encouragement, and faith, and you have demonstrated that there is no matter, evil, disease, or death.

Now, "loose him and let him go." Take your anxious thought off the condition and release it in God. And do not look back to see how things are going. They are going in the right direction, and regardless of what you may see or hear, they still are going in the right direction. They always do, when we let go and *let* God. Ancestry does not govern us. We are entirely God governed. Any attempt on your part or mine to steer the ship is taking away from God's right to maintain his own image and likeness. Parents do not manufacture a body, a brain, or a mind for their children. You would not know how to even create a fingernail should one be needed. And the body did not create itself—the body is not self-acting. The power we call God, life, mind, spirit, Soul, it did the creating, and it does the maintaining and sustaining. "The mind of the individual only can produce a result upon his body,"[14] and what is this mind of the individual but God. Now, the mind of us embodies, includes within itself and expresses infinite God power, and I ask you to rest and to trust this great mind of the individual, which is God.

Any mortal picture temporarily present, you must disregard until God reveals to you the perfect picture, which even this minute stands where "sinning mortal man appears to mortals." You will never see the perfect, or spiritual man through material sense, so do not try. As you learn to turn from material sense, your spiritual vision grows, and through this spiritual sense you behold reality.

～

The sole aim of our work is the realization of the presence and power of God. "I can of mine own self do nothing,"[15] is literally true, but the fact remains that "the Father that dwelleth in me, he doeth the works."[16] Rather, it is the *consciousness of the presence of the Father within* that does the work. How may we become conscious of the presence of the Father? By stilling the human senses and listening for the "still, small voice." Our attitude must always be "listening" for that voice. Then, I would say that our two important words are "receptivity" and "reflection." Let us become receptive to the divine ideas, and then let us reflect on them as they appear.

Health and harmony are conditions of mind and therefore universal and omnipresent. As we then become "still" and dwell on thoughts of love and peace, the divine "peace, that passeth understanding" comes to us and brings a sense of health and harmony. We must spend several periods each day in quiet contemplation, in receptive reflection, in meditation. Over and over we must joyously entreat, "Speak, Lord; for thy servant heareth" and "I will listen for thy voice." This is so important. Not the words, the affirmations, the denials that we speak are power, but the Word of God which comes to us from mind.

Healing is not difficult when we once know that we are not trying to heal a body or improve man or change him, but that we are trying only to establish in our consciousness the awareness of the peace that is already there, awaiting our recognition. Then, let us take "peace, be still" for our Word, let us "seek peace" within us; let us realize the presence of peace in our consciousness. In the silence of the night when you are awake, realize peace within you. Peace is a great healer. Do not seek healing, seek peace; the healing is the "added thing."

The great healer is the sense of peace you find within your own consciousness. We do not need words or thoughts, because as our Master asked, "Which of you by taking thought can add one cubit unto his stature?"[17] "Take no thought," because "your Father knoweth that ye have need of these things" and "it is your Father's good pleasure to give you the kingdom."[18]

If, at times, thought will not be still, the senses will not quiet, then dwell on peace, quietness, stillness, until material sense is still, and the ideas of God become perfectly tangible and real. This is to experience the Christ.

⁓

The divine mind, which is the mind of the individual governs and controls every phase of his existence, even in the physical realm, so-called. Every organ of the body, every function, all action, is harmoniously governed by this mind, your mind. No other mind nor the thought from any one or any group has any jurisdiction over your affairs or mine. The *belief* that any other mind has power in your individual experience must be cast out of your thought. Your life experience, including your health, is the direct product of your mind, which is God, or infinite good. Any error in your body or health—that is, any error seeming or claiming to be in the body—is actually not there, but exists merely as illusion, as mesmerism, due to ignorance of the truth of being. Your body is the perfect manifestation of your mind, which is God, and therefore expresses all the qualities and activity of perfection, and any other appearance is illusion. Nothing that exists in the realm of effect can affect your health, harmony, body, or being. Food, weather, climate, germs, bullets—anything outside yourself—are inert and powerless to control you. Even your own body has no life, intelligence, action of its own, but reflects the life and action of mind, your mind.

The body cannot contract a disease or manifest one. The body cannot act or refuse to act; it cannot digest or refuse to digest. All action, digestion, assimilation, and elimination are activities of mind, which the body automatically reflects. We never suffer from any effect: poison, germ, weather, etc., but only from the *belief* that these have power to cause evil conditions. Give up the belief that anything but the mind of the individual has power, and you will live forever in health and peace. The body cannot change, age, or run down, and the *belief* that the body has such power must be given up.

You are the law unto yourself through this understanding and in no other way. Your own mind having or embodying infinite God power, is sufficient to break every illusion. Do remember, whatever of discord may be in evidence *has no existence,* but is merely illusion or mesmerism or hypnotism, and to know this, dispels the illusion—de-hypnotizes. Never fear a discordant condition regardless of what its appearance is to sense. The appearance has no power. Know that the body has no intelligence, has no sensation and cannot feel pain. If the body cannot think, it cannot feel.

~

"Arise, shine; for thy light is come."[19] Thy light is recognized as here and now. "Lazarus, (divine being) come forth"[20]—out of the tomb of human belief, come into the light of the recognition of your divine life, here and now. Take off the "grave clothes" of superstition and of belief of mortal selfhood. "Loose him" from the bondage of fear and doubt, and set him free to realize and experience the freedom of life, God, your life.

"One with God is a majority" and the mind that was in Christ Jesus (my mind) calls *you* into the freedom of eternal life here and now. "I say unto thee, arise,"[21] and as "I" call unto the divinity of your being, the shackles of sin, fear, disease, and death fall to the ground—become nothingness.

"Cease ye from (being a) man whose breath is in his nostrils"[22] and be that which you are. "I and my Father are one"[23]—you are not a mortal, nor a human being. "Thou shalt have no other gods before me."[24] Thou shalt recognize spirit only as creator, Father, and therefore the son, made in his image and likeness, as spiritual. "The life was the light of men"[25] shows clearly that his life is the life of man, indestructible, indivisible, whole; his mind is the mind of man, and so understands and expresses the truth of harmonious being.

You must see the whole garment; his life as your life; his mind as your mind; his being as your being; and only then do you realize that "I and my Father are one"—one life, one mind, one being, and one body, embodying every quality and activity of infinite being.

Behind the desire for bigger practice is the belief that there are sick people who need healing, or that there are those who need the light of truth to replace the darkness of ignorance. This belief must be corrected in your thought, because the belief you hold of others' sicknesses and needs reacts upon you only. I have learned that there is no malpractice except self-malpractice. It is impossible for another to be injured by our wrong concepts, just as our ignorance of mathematics does not injure or limit another. "Let your light so shine" means to hold steadfastly to the truth that man (all men) is the individual expression of God; that God is individual mind, therefore, the mind of every individual, and so there is not in all heaven and earth a sick, sinful, or ignorant man. In fact, the absolute truth is that there is not God and man, but God expressed as man. How can God be sick or sinful?

This is the reason you never give your treatment to man, but always know the truth about God, because the truth you know about God, is the truth about God manifested, which is individual being called man.

When the desire for greater practice comes to you, reverse it immediately by knowing that the only practice is the activity or understanding of truth, God, and you are the infinite expression of that practice. All desire must be reversed as soon as it appears with the truth that, because of omnipresence, fulfillment is the law, and right where the desire appears, there fulfillment is.

Never allow a desire to remain in thought, or you will continue demonstrating desire. But if you realize immediately that right where desire claims to be, there is fulfillment, you will demonstrate (prove) fulfillment. Why is this true? Because mind and its manifestation is one, and whatever you hold in mind is instantly manifested. Now, the practice of truth is the infinite omnipresent activity of mind (your mind, the only mind) and your constant recognition of this truth results in joyous, fruitful activity. This activity is not healing the sick, it is the continuous recognition that "mind is not sick and matter cannot be;"[26] that life is not sick and therefore the expression cannot be sick. All that mind, life is, the manifestation of life, mind, is.

The desire to heal is *human* good. The realization of the spiritual nature and character of man is *spiritual* practice.

~ 14 ~

FAITH

Should you hope? How different from the woman who asked Jesus to heal her daughter and was refused! Through her persistence, she finally received the gift of healing.

Let me start by telling you the first thing you must do is to agree to see the problem objectively, that is, as something out there which does not belong to you. We must learn to give up self, whether it comes in the form of self-pity, self-righteousness, or any of the other phases of self. As a matter of fact, any good that you have done in the world was not done by you, really, nor is it to your credit. God manifests his goodness to the world and we are his offspring, so that all credit for all good belongs solely to him.

Truth heals. If you have seen it work only a few times, you know that it does. Is any form of error an actual condition? You know that it is nothing but a suggestion or appearance. It is, therefore, mental and can be met with the knowing of the truth about God and man. When you see converging rails, does it mean that here is a physical condition of discord and that the rails must be physically separated again? No, you *know* that this is an appearance or suggestion and cannot be met physically. It must be met mentally by knowing the truth about the situation.

The body is not sick. Matter does not pain. Eyes do not see. These are mental arguments and must be refuted with the truth about God and man or, rather, with the understanding that what appears as man is mind manifested. Therefore, what is this discord or disease but appearance or argument? Error comes to individual thought as suggestion or argument and it is there that it must be met. Remember, error is never in the other person; it comes to your thought or my thought. We either accept it as a reality, or reject it for the lying argument that it is. Do not ask any whys at this point, but accept it as fact, put it into immediate practice without a single question and hold steadfastly without wavering—no question, no doubt, no fear—but consistent holding to this truth, until your consciousness is full to overflowing with joy, gratitude, and love for its verity, and you will see the fruitage.

You see we must take our stand on the truth that there is but one God, or creative principle, and that there can, therefore, be no effect from any other cause. God alone is cause, and all else exists as effect. God is the only law unto all effects, and no one effect has *any* power or jurisdiction over another effect.

Why fear that which has neither presence, nor power? Jesus was asked of Pilate: "Knowest thou not that I have power to crucify thee, and have power to release thee?"[1] And Jesus answered: "Thou couldst have no power at all against me, except it were given thee from above."[2] He knew that error was not power, because *good* alone is power.

There is only spiritual man, who exists as consciousness. In this consciousness exist complete, and completely manifested, all ideas of mind. As we lay off our material beliefs, we become aware of their presence as a divine reality. You must work the healing out in your own consciousness with no regard for what anyone thinks, says, or does; and with no concern on your part. *Let* it come, do not give it thought, whether or not it be slow or fast, but work it out within yourself. You have much ahead of you when you learn to impersonalize the "I".

~ 15 ~

ONE INFINITE LIFE

We speak of "your" life, "my" life, or "his" or "her" life, whereas it is necessary for us to remember that there is in all the world only *one* life. This life is deathless, ageless, diseaseless, and changeless; it is the individual expression of that *one* divine life. In other words, our life is divine life individualized. It contains no element of matter, discord or inharmony, no decomposition or decrepitude. This life, of which we are the individual expression, is composed of the substance of spirit, is infinite, eternal and harmonious.

"He that seeth me seeth him that sent me."[1]

Whether we speak of you or me, we are speaking of divine life, individually expressed in all its harmony and perfection. This life is mind, and the faculties of mind are universally and impartially expressed through all of mind's ideas. Its faculties are never dependent on material conditions, or circumstances of birth, age or maturity. So let us learn to drop the "my" life, "my" vision, "my" understanding, "my" supply, and think in terms of life, vision, understanding and supply; and all of these as individually expressed through you and me. Intelligence, wisdom, vision, power, are not personal, but are impersonal, impartial and universal.

In a universe governed by divine principle, man never leaves his state of peace, harmony, health and security. The law of spirit, divine principle, maintains man forever in his rightful place and condition of being. There are no material states or stages of consciousness for there is but one consciousness–spiritual consciousness–in which there is neither matter nor material beliefs. This is our only consciousness; there is no material substance, no material body, and in this consciousness man is found spiritual, incorporeal, harmonious and complete.

Health, harmony, wholeness, is the direct result of consciousness. It is not dependent on mental manipulation but on our consciousness of the harmony, peace and freedom of all God's universe. As we perceive that the principle of life can only express itself harmoniously, completely and impartially, it is so unto us and we bring it into our human experience.

Errors are but shadows of belief thrown out by human thought onto the screen of visible form. There is in reality no error. Error has no substance, no body, no form, no law to enforce it, no mind to create it, express or respond to it. Error has no channel for its transmission. It has no memory, and is without power to perpetuate itself. It has no existence apart from the false belief that is at the moment sustaining it. If our thought continues permeated with truth from the Bible or inspired metaphysical writings, these truths will take the place formerly occupied by false beliefs. The revelation of the perfect man will come about in natural ways "not by might, nor by power, but by my spirit,"[2] and we may rest assured that "the words that I speak unto you, they are spirit, and they are life." The very thoughts that keep coming to us, these constitute the Word. Thus, we should continue to know that all activity is not personal, but impersonal, universal and impartial, and that the

~130~

activity of good, God, is infinitely expressed in us, as it is in every divine idea.

We learn to devote some part of every day to communion with God. While striving to obey the Scriptural injunction to "pray without ceasing," we find it helpful to set aside specific moments in which to silently receive the influx of divine ideas, God's thoughts. Before retiring at night, it is well to have sufficient time of quiet in which to realize a great sense of peace. In these moments, we seek the assurance of God's presence, our atonement, and a sense of spiritual freedom.

"For thus saith the Lord God, the Holy One of Israel; In returning and rest shall ye be saved; in quietness and confidence shall be your strength."[3]

"Seek ye first the Kingdom of God, and his righteousness; and all these things shall be added unto you."[4]

This may seem to be one of the most difficult statements to understand or demonstrate until we know what "the kingdom of God" is and how to seek it. Now, the kingdom of God is that state of consciousness wherein all is peace and harmony. Therefore, when we have attained a sense of peace and harmony, we may know that we are in the kingdom of God, and that "all these things" are being added unto us: health, wealth, activity, business, wholeness, holiness, freedom, joy and eternal bliss. When we retire at night with a complete feeling of his presence in us—"in his holy temple"—then our rest cannot be invaded.

If we begin each new day with a short period of quiet in which to feel God's love permeating us, God's spirit empowering us we can know that throughout the day, his thoughts will be expressed through us, since he "declareth unto man what is his thought." We can know that we will utter only his words, which are words of truth and power, hearing only what his ear hears, because his presence shuts out mortal hearing and believing. We will understand and know with his mind if we acknowledge that God is the only mind we have, receiving and responding only to all things good. Realizing that his presence is power, we will know that every detail of our lives, every judgment, every action, every thought and move we make throughout the day will be of him, manifesting through us. We will then see that there is no selfhood apart from God.

~ 16 ~

WITHIN-NESS

Are you in the mood to write? Yes? Then, the inspiration will be provided for you, because there is inherent in the human consciousness that which serves when the need arises.

What is there in man that writes? What is there in the Soul of man that pushes itself out into manifestation or expression? What is the nature of this infinite source of all knowledge that pours itself through the fingers of men? Is there nothing of this to be known but that it is; that it does force itself into the minds of men and thus gives the world new beauties of thought, new facets of life, new ideals to live up to?

The intelligent nature of this fount of all inspiration indicates a definite plan in the progression with which ideas reveal themselves to individual thought.

The capacity of man to receive is the measure of his capacity to give, to unfold, reveal, or to write. The creative urge is but the ability to listen to the "still, small voice" of eternal mind, and this "listening" brings forth, likewise, the power of expression.

The loveliness of thought unfolded to the world in the writings of the immortals is but the revelation of the harmonies of heaven sent to the hearts of men to lighten the path of human existence.

Again, the capacity of men to understand and to appreciate these gems of brilliant thought is the measure of their joy and prosperity in the midst of the mental poverty and earthly sorrow of mortals.

"Silver and gold have I none," says the consciousness of perfect being, "but the ideals of eternity I make practical for you in the harmony of your being, therefore, take up that bed of physical and moral infirmity and walk in health of mind and body." "Receive these truths and be free of ignorance, fear and woe," is the invitation of the masters of inspiration.

~ 17 ~

LETTER AND SPIRIT OF TRUTH

The world is always presenting to us pictures of sin, disease, discord, lack, and limitation. Ignorance of the truth of being causes us to accept these pictures at face value, instead of translating them back into terms of God's actual creation. Only the study of truth reveals that these pictures are but false concepts of reality; that underlying these false views of life, there is the universe of God's creating. We know now that it is sacrilegious to claim that there is a God, an infinite power, and that there is discord too. It just does not make sense. Either there *is* God, infinite and eternal, universal and impartial, and therefore only perfection; or there is no God, and chaos, confusion, and lack of control are actualities. Assuming God, one must be logical and assume a universe intelligently and lovingly and harmoniously governed, controlled, maintained, and sustained.

Then where do these pictures and evidences of discord come from? They emanate from thousands of years of accumulated beliefs in a selfhood apart from God. These beliefs constitute a state of deception or mesmerism through which we see and experience that which has no actual or externalized existence, namely an illusion. A hypnotized person may be made to chase a dog–a non-existent dog–but one which in the mesmerized state *seems* real. We can never remove the dog from the scene because he isn't there. But when we can convey to the hypnotized man that the dog exists only as illusion, he awakens from his dream.

In the degree that you and I see that all corporeal existence (even so-called healthy corporeal existence) is but an illusion of human or mesmeric sense, we too awaken from the beliefs in a selfhood apart from God. God is your life, your mind, your being, the substance of your body, and therefore, you are actually entirely spiritual. All that appears as material is the illusion or false sense of self, produced by the age-old and universal aggregation of beliefs which constitute the universal mesmerism.

However, right here we must remember that the human understanding of these facts is not always sufficient. Sometimes healing does come through the intellectual statement or continuous affirmation of these truths. But often another step is necessary: the spiritual realization of truth, an inner awareness or conviction of these things; and the lack of this accounts for delayed healings. Either the constant affirmation and firm refusal to admit the claims of error has not been adhered to, or thought has not yet given way to spiritual sense.

We look upon thought as an avenue of awareness. Through thought we become aware of that which is. We do not use thought to make it happen.

~

My previous letters were introductions to the main theme which will run like a thread through all that follows. It is always the spirit or consciousness of truth, that establishes us in the Way. " It is God that establishes us in Christ". St. Paul

But some measure of the letter of Science is also necessary, and so in my last letters I have tried to give you briefly what I understand to be the letter of truth; namely, one mind, God, and that mind the mind of the individual; that mind, all good, producing all and only good on the body, business, home. The same truth always applies to health, body, home, supply, work, etc. There are not separate lists of truth for various problems; there is only one truth and its infinite manifestation. Next, that error, regardless of form, name, nature, character, or degree, is illusion. And the *only* way to handle illusion is to recognize it as such. Having done that, you have done all. From then on, stand and stand fast, permitting no other thoughts or arguments to have room in your consciousness. It must be thoroughly understood within you that all intelligence, action, substance, law, cause, and reality are mind, manifesting as effect and that no life, intelligence, action, substance, are in the effect as such, but always in the cause or principle. In other words, bowels do not move: mind moves and bowels reflect this movement; blood does not circulate and the heart does not beat. Only mind acts. "Because matter has no consciousness or Ego, it cannot act; its conditions are illusions."[1] "And why not, since Mind, God, is the source and condition of all existence?"[2]

As we "get" this into our consciousness, we learn how impossible it is to fear the lungs, heart, blood, germs, fever, or bombs. And when we lose the fear of the body we have gained immortal life. Only fear of the body causes death, and there is no way to stop fearing it until we arrive at the understanding that the body is not self-acting and that it obeys the dictates of mind–our own infinite mind or spiritual consciousness. I call this process learning to withdraw thought from the objective realm or world of effect. It is drawing our attention back into the kingdom within us.

We make now a natural transition in the line of light to a radical reliance on the spirit of truth. In the final test, our good comes to us, "not by might, nor by power, but by my spirit."[3]

Material sense will never reveal the perfect or spiritual man. We behold "the perfect man" in proportion to our ability to lay off the reasoning being and become the intuitive being. "Reason is the most active human faculty."[4] Note that *human* faculty. Intuition is the spiritual faculty; it is a spiritual quality. Pure mind does not reason, but it reveals that which is. And we develop this spiritual faculty as we learn to put off the old man who judges by appearances, gain the new man who intuitively perceives the reality behind the mask of personality.

~ 18 ~

SEARCH FOR FREEDOM

The uncertainties of human existence compel us to seek a way out of the difficulties that so frequently beset us. Illnesses of every name and nature mark our lives from infancy to old age; failure, disappointments, lack, and limitation seem to be our lot, even though each new year finds us hoping for a healthier and happier one than ever before, and as each "old year" passes we have but few regrets.

Inherently we know that this should not be. Indeed, we become more certain with each disappointment that it need not be. Somewhere, we feel, is freedom from mortal trials and human tribulations. We know this freedom can be gained, if we but learn the way.

Every human breast prays to God—perhaps to an "unknown God"—for the answer. Every nation and every race looks to its conception of the Almighty for rest, peace, and surcease from its worldly cares. The answer can only be found in God, the one true God whom Jesus called "our Father."

In the degree that we understand God and his government of the universe, we are enabled to bring ourselves into harmony with the laws of spirit, under the jurisdiction of divine mind, and we find that every phase of human life is directly maintained in harmony and perfection through the reign of truth."

It is our ignorance of God, the divine principle, which produces apparent discord, and the right understanding of him restores harmony."[1]

In Christian Science we find that God is divine mind and, therefore, its creation must be in the form of ideas; that God is principle and his government must necessarily be impersonal, impartial, and universal; that God is love and this divine quality is manifested in the care and protection of love's creation; that God is truth, expressing infinite wisdom in its control over man and the universe; that God is spirit, the eternal, unchanging substance of all being. Added to these, we learn that God is infinite life, the one and only life, animating all men and things.

Continuing our study of the Bible in order to find the key to healthful and successful living, we learn that God is the one and only creator, and that, therefore, his creation must inevitably express the qualities of his perfect being. Man, the "expression of God's being," is forever reflecting the universal government of principle, the infinite wisdom of mind, and the care and protection of divine love. He must necessarily manifest the unchanging qualities of spirit and enjoy God's unlimited substance. Therefore, man's life is the eternal expression and manifestation of the one universal divine life.

These truths are self-evident and assure us that, since in spirit there is no matter; in divine life there is no death; in principle there is neither change nor accident; in truth there is no error; that in man, God's image and likeness, there cannot be found one single element of destruction, nor one negative tract or quality.

Our Master, Christ Jesus, declared, ". . . know the truth, and the truth shall make you free."[2] When we consciously know the truth about God and man, and also of the relationship which exists between the divine Father and the Son of God, this understanding automatically frees us from the limiting beliefs responsible for discordant conditions of so-called material existence.

In divine Science we learn there is but one universal consciousness, in which is embodied the entire universe, including every idea and manifestation. This consciousness is the only creator and is infinite and eternal. It is, therefore, forever conscious of each and every created being and thing, *"from the infinitesimal to the infinite,"* and since this is true, no person or thing can drop from consciousness or lapse into unconsciousness, either temporarily or permanently.

The divine universal consciousness contains within itself, as well as maintains, the identity of all—*"from a blade of grass to a star."* We need not look to any individual to maintain his own consciousness or another's; nor need we labor to attain a consciousness of health, home, beauty, supply, etc., because these are infinite, ever-present ideas—forms of creation—eternally established and supported in this consciousness we call God, and forever expressed through the individual consciousness receptive and responsive to his Word.

Man is already established, supported, and healthfully maintained in this consciousness, together with every other idea necessary to the completion and perfection of him as the infinite Son.

The permanency of individual life and the consciousness of all good is a surety throughout our earthly experience; not by virtue of the effort, labor or will of individual man, but by the recognition that as long as divine consciousness *is*, man is, because he is the individualized expression of every quality of the infinite and eternal divine consciousness, God.

As we apprehend the truth that divine consciousness, universal mind, can express itself only as spiritual ideas, that man is the greatest of these, with dominion over all lesser ideas, we lose the false sense of material existence with its material limitations. Also, losing the material sense of life, we gain the spiritual consciousness in which we find that eternal life and its expression is one; that every quality of divine life, truth, and love is expressed in every individual life, for every life is the perfect expression of the harmony and peace of God's being.

~ 19 ~

True Desires

Our desires are usually for something external to us and hinder our obedience to the Scriptural injunction to, "Seek ye first the Kingdom of God and his righteousness."[1]

We must lose all desire for and drop all thought of externals, whether of place, position, person, thing, or condition. Instead of these we are to desire spiritual realities: love, harmony, peace, confidence, understanding, truth.

> "Finally, brethren, whatsoever things are true, whatsoever things are honest, whatsoever things are just, whatsoever things are pure, whatsoever things are lovely, whatsoever things are of good report, if there be any virtue, and if there be any praise, think on these things."[2]
>
> Paul

As we appreciate these qualities we are seeking first "the kingdom of God," and as we gain an understanding of them, our human conditions become the very expression of good in all ways. Are we seeking health? We seek amiss. Our desire (prayer) should be for the consciousness of perfection to become conscious of harmony, peace, order, life, truth and love. In this consciousness there is no element of discord, inharmony, or disease.

Are we seeking money with which to pay our bills? We seek amiss. Our desire (prayer) should be for the mind which was also in Christ Jesus, the mind which knows that "Every good gift and every perfect gift is from above, and cometh down from the Father,"[3] and "All that the Father giveth me shall come to me."[4] We need to strive for the consciousness of ever-present abundance, of love fulfilling every need. We must turn away from the temptation to think in terms of externals, of bills, debts, material needs, lack, or limitation. Holding persistently to spiritual realities will fulfill all needs, both of a spiritual and material nature.

We can lose the belief of unemployment in the consciousness that mind is forever occupied with spiritual activity, and that mind is continuously expressing this activity through individual consciousness. Keeping thought in line with spiritual activity, with no thought or fear of the external condition, will unfailingly result in the harmonious and fruitful outward expression of useful and profitable employment.

Spiritual desire is prayer, and true prayer is a law of fulfillment of every human need. Desire (prayer) for truth and love is desire for Christ, and this Christ is the manifestation of God's being, or the activity of good which fulfills all desires, answers all prayer.

The urge to desire or pray for spiritual good, for spiritual understanding, for spiritual qualities, and then be tempted to think of these in terms of externals must be overcome. Matter and material conditions are not the realities of being. They do not constitute our real life. To give thought, therefore, to either the material condition or the channels through which good may come, is to have thought on that which is not real and which is without power or presence. It is evidence of doubt or fear that the spiritual may not be all power, all presence, all reality. This is doubt of God, which is the greatest of all sins.

"Take no thought for your life, what ye shall eat; neither for the body, what ye shall put on. . . . If ye then be not able to do that thing which is least, why take ye thought for the rest?"[5]

~ 20 ~

PROBLEMS

In the working out of a problem, it would seem to me that the first step would be to forget yourself and the problem as it appears and study more about the universal nature of good.

As you begin to look away from self and personal problems and dwell more in thought on the universality of 2x2 being 4, or do, re, mi following each other, and of the law of "like begetting like," you will see how impossible it would be for you to be anywhere outside of divine law, divine protection, and divine action.

When we plant a rose seed we know, of course, that only a rose can come forth. We do not go into any ecstasies of delight about the wonders of the rose seed because we know that it is not the rose seed itself that produced the rose, but the law of "like begetting like" acting upon the seed.

Planting the seed in fertile soil, giving it sufficient water and sun, the rose is inevitable, and even the seed itself could not prevent the fulfillment. Also, when we place 2 and 2 together, 4 is inevitable, and this is not by any virtue of the objects or numbers that are brought together, but because of the operation of the law of mathematics.

These illustrations apply to us in like manner. Divine law governs its creations. The only God there is, is principle, the principle of our being, and it would be impossible for our affairs to get outside the operation of this law. Then all the error, inharmony, discord, that is apparent to us is, as a matter of fact, not present at all, but exists only as belief and must be so understood.

A belief operates as a law only until its true nature is discerned, just as the belief that 3 x 3 is 8 vanishes without any further effort on our part. We do not have to destroy it or rise above it, because it vanishes of its own nothingness, its non-existence.

~

Let us know that "whatsoever God doeth, it shall be for ever;"[1] that there is not a single element of error, discord, inharmony or fear in either God or his son, in mind or its idea, in spirit or its manifestation, in life or its expression; because spirit, God, is all and there is no matter.

Consciously know the truth every time a thought comes to you. As you keep thought away from the seeming problem (in the sense of continual self-treatment), it will be easier for you to receive the messages mind conveys to you. Know and be conscious always that only God, good, has presence or power, and see God in everything.

As you see the trees and flowers come into blossom, know that life, God, is manifesting Self in these signs of life, and just so is life, harmony, eternally manifesting itself as you. The change from material belief to spiritual understanding is a painless and normal advance. The unfoldment or revelation of Christ, truth, the only man there is is natural, serene, harmonious, painless, perfect.

There is no discord in spirit. Become conscious that, "spirit and its formations are the only realities of being,"[2] and nothing else is present or has power. Truth does reveal itself to the receptive thought. It is essential that you personally spend time on seeking a consciousness, or sense of peace, as well as reading and studying. If you will frequently retire to a corner, away from people, compose yourself, take your thought off human affairs, and seek a state of peace, a whole new life will open up to you.

This is a gradual process, because human thought seeks to be active, to declare truths, to stop pain, to worry. And always it seeks to do these things through some form of mental activity! Cultivate moments of silence with a "peace, be still," or "be still, and know that I am God," or just "peace." The silence will result in a sense of calm and peace which will enable you to see the problem in its right light, and this consciousness will solve it for you.

It is more difficult to be silent than to declare truths, and for that reason more effort should be made to accomplish it. You may not at first see the good it has done for you, but you will bless the effort you have made to learn the joy and calm of "peace, be still."

Jesus did not have to speak to the wind and waters; he merely sought the mental calm of his own thought and the waters reflected the calm of his consciousness.

This I have learned: we can know a constant flow of harmonious human experience as the *outflow* of the morning's receptivity and reflection. The day's activities are the direct result of this spiritual inflow. It is difficult in language to hook up a spiritual sense with a human job, or physical health or economic well being, but there is a definite connection. Dwelling on the impersonal sense of "I" is a big help.

～

Disease does not exist as a physical condition. It is the externalization of thought or belief. Mind governs and directs thought in its rightful channel, correcting belief; thus showing forth harmonious objectification or effect.

You co-exist with mind, consciousness—the principle of thought. This makes you free to mold thought and its expression in perfect harmony. Therefore, you are the thinker, the cause or creator of your thought and as such you must co-exist with mind, principle. Unless you see this you will always be looking for a power or presence apart from yourself to act upon you, upon your thinking, or your affairs; in which case you will (in belief) have separated yourself from the one and only God, cause or creator, your divine Self, the only Self, the One.

Do not let this shock you. You are taught to follow the teaching of Christ Jesus, and his teaching declares: "I am the way, the truth, and the life;"[3] "I am the resurrection and the life;"[4] "He that seeth me seeth him that sent me;"[5] he "said also that God was his Father, making himself equal with God."[6] And Paul spoke of him thus, "Who, being in the form of God, thought it not robbery to be equal with God."[7] You must believe this!

Manifestation, body, business, health, home, can never be separate from thought, because they are the outward expressions of your thought or conscious awareness. To manifest perfect body, being, health, harmony, it is necessary to know that you, the source of your thought (the thinker) is ever maintaining the purity and truth of your thinking in righteous channels. If you look to a power apart from yourself to govern or control you, it does not make any difference whether or not you bow down to a brass monkey or a God in the heavens. Nothing of which you can conceive as God is God, because the conceiver must always be greater than his conception; the thinker is always greater than his thoughts and no presence or power can govern thought except the thinker.

Know, therefore, that as the thinker, co-existing with mind, truth is the substance of your thought as well as of its manifestation; that principle maintains and sustains the integrity of your thinking and of its effects. Thus you become captain of your ship, the master of your fate. All true teaching is based on this premise and all revelation confirms it. When you have learned to live as consciousness, bit by bit you will discover that all the universe is the expression, the manifestation of this consciousness which you are, and that your universe is subject to this conscious awareness.

The invitation reads: "Come out . . . and be ye separate,"[8] and in the degree that we come out from our material thoughts, human interests, we are able to become aware of the fact that we are truth itself in manifestation. Truth, as you know, is infinite. Therefore, can you imagine "getting" infinity? What could contain infinity? What would be the nature of that which could possess infinity or truth? Rather, must we see that we co-exist with mind as truth. We cannot have truth, that would be twoness, but to co-exist with mind as truth is oneness. To state or know this is of little benefit. We must live it, and live it until we have the actual awareness, the spiritual consciousness of its *is*-ness. Then only are we free of the belief of separation, of two-ness.

~

In human experience we are continually being faced with what appears to be discordant conditions and persons. This has always been so. Jesus was faced with a Judas. Moses withdrew his hand from his bosom to find it covered with leprosy. Then came the discovery that there is no disease, no sin, no sick people, and no sinner. Among the truths that led to this discovery was the Bible statement: "All things were made by him; and without him was not any thing made that was made,"[9] and "God saw every thing that he had made, and, behold, it was very good."[10]

It must follow that in this universe there is no error, neither sin, disease, nor death. And this being true, wherever such discords appear, they are not in the universe, but in our false concept of the universe. I illustrate this thus: If you were to walk into your parlor and see a ghost, your first reaction would be one of fright. Someone beside you would say, "Don't be afraid, that is not a ghost," but you would still be fearful; then he would say, "That's a piece of furniture I covered with a sheet." You would quickly see that there was nothing to fear; that which appeared to you as a ghost or evil was something natural and right, merely taking on an erroneous form in your mind. With the correction the complete healing would take place.

Our work consists of getting a sense of harmony or at-one-ment and then letting this consciousness of peace do the work. This consciousness is attained by the study, application, and proof of the basic truths of being, namely, that "There is no life, truth, intelligence, nor substance in matter. All is infinite mind and its infinite manifestation;"[11] that "The real jurisdiction of the world is in mind, controlling every effect;"[12] that "Christ, or the spiritual idea, appeared to human consciousness as the man Jesus."[13] This is the true being of every individual. That which I am seeking, I am; meaning that as consciousness I embody, embrace, include within myself, within my consciousness "the fulness of the Godhead, bodily"; that as mind manifest, I include within myself every right idea of life, substance, reality.

It becomes necessary to frequently remind ourselves of these and other basic truths as they unfold. We either consciously or unconsciously build a consciousness of truth that is based on what we have read, studied, practiced, and have had revealed to us through individual revelation. We are the sum total of all these experiences and this demonstrated consciousness heals and teaches for you, for me, and for those who have applied themselves in this manner.

We cannot accept a God who rewards or punishes, yet we must accept a principle which, if conformed to, reveals harmony and which, if not conformed to, results in discord. We cannot accept a God who makes exceptions, or who in any way sets aside divine law for any reason.

There are no discordant conditions. Perfection is the reality of being, and any appearance to the contrary is a false concept of perfection, harmony, and true being.

~

Someone told me once that patience was that quality of mind that can look through seeming discord and see the completed demonstration. You can see that if we can look through discord, we no longer need to have patience, because if we can see the completed demonstration, we are not fooled by the appearance of the moment. We are called on to come to the point where we are convinced that illusions are no more mental than they are physical. An illusion is an illusion whether it be mental or physical, and an illusion cannot be objectified.

It *is* divine love that meets every human need, but it is the divine love that we express, and not a divine love off somewhere in the vault of blue.

The bodily ill for the moment is what drives us on until we learn that we never really were seeking just health, but were all the time struggling to reach some measure of understanding God. Without these ills of mind, body, or purse, we would be content to go on living in the material sense of things, until one day old age would be upon us before we realized it, and then it might take some later awakening to bring us "home" to the consciousness of heaven here and now.

It is becoming clearer that all bodily discord is embraced in the material sense of existence, and that spiritual sense is the reality of all things. It is not the universe doing anything to us, but our sense of the universe is reflecting itself back to us. If we have a spiritual sense of man and the universe we perceive the spiritual in all men and things and they reflect themselves back to us as spiritual harmony. If we entertain a material sense of the world, it reflects a false sense back to us, known as sin, disease, death, lack.

All harmony is included in the spiritual sense of life and the universe. There is no change in the so-called outer universe involved; it is but the change of our concept of man and the universe. No change ever takes place in the world, in our affairs, in our bodies; all the change takes place in our consciousness of the world, of our affairs, of our bodies.

This is a step closer to the vision of St. John: a city in which is no structural edifice and, yet, it is tangible and real to spiritual sense. For many years we used Christian Science like we formerly used doctors, medicine, and surgery as a curative or preventative agency. Also for years, we used it as a comforting religion, "getting our good" from services, lectures, and books. Ultimately the call comes to rise higher.

It is at this point that we realize that truth is the revelation of God which, when understood, includes all harmony or, as Jesus speaks of it, "these things shall be added unto you." When? When you have found the kingdom of God.

You are entitled to health, harmony, healing, here and now. In fact, you have all these right now and this revelation of Christian Science is showing to you your perfect selfhood, here and now. Our work is to bring more than physical healing; it is to awaken in you the spiritual sense of life, the consciousness which can behold the universe of God's creating, that universe of which it is written, "there shall be no night there." Isn't it a glorious path that lies before us?

~21~

BUSINESS

This is a word on *business:* "Ye shall know the truth, and the truth shall make you free,"[1] and the truth that you must know is that you are already free.

All business is God's business regardless of its nature. The only food there is, is the "bread of life" which God alone serves; the only water is the "water of life" which freely flows from God to man, and the wine of inspiration which has its fount in heaven. God supplies all these to his children (receptive thoughts), that he may be fully expressed.

Drop the weight of responsibility from your shoulders. "Stand ye still" and let love provide the customers, the volume, and the profits. Allow no thought of competition to enter. You are not dependent on material conditions for your business. The lie of mortal mind is that you are dependent on weather, prosperity, surroundings, or no competition for your success. On the contrary, these are human thoughts and they are the weights which must be put aside. We are told to "lay aside every weight . . . which doth so easily beset us."[2]

Prepare thought for the day's business and mentally invite the world. Know that love fills all space, that every corner of your world is filled with divine ideas that express joy, gratitude, and love. Keep thought away from transactions. Just hold to the truth that Christ has invited all to "come unto me"–be served of him. Do not give or receive "treatments" for the success of business, but know constantly that divine intelligence is continually expressing *itself* in your business; that divine love is eternally being manifested in it; that mind produces all the needed activity; that love supplies the currency; that principle is forever expressing itself in harmonious, active, and complete business. Let no thought of conditions, weather, competition, enter to mar your faith and trust in the fact that truth is now expressed as your business. As a matter of fact, truth is your only business, the embodiment of harmony, complete life, and permanent action. Keep thought filled with the truth that it is God-governed and God-supported.

There is no element of evil in your business, no element of lack or limitation. The seeming absence of activity is not a lack of God or good, not an element of evil. It is God knocking at the door of your consciousness telling you to "lift up your eyes, and look on the fields; for they are white already to harvest;"[3] see that your salvation is not dependent on man or material conditions and place your faith and trust in the power of the ever-present law of mind to express itself in harmony and abundance.

Worry is distrust of the principle, lack of faith in omnipotent power. Neither of these are a part of your consciousness, nor have they presence or power anywhere or at any time. Fears or worries have not the power to hold back the hand of omnipotence. Regardless of these you are individual consciousness where the harmonious activity of continuous business is forever experienced. "Creation (business) is ever appearing, and must ever continue to appear from the nature of its inexhaustible source."[4] This is true business. Study II Kings 25:29-30. "And he did eat bread continually before him all the days of his life. And his allowance was a continual allowance given him of the king, a daily rate for every day, all the days of his life."

There is no selfhood apart from God, no body, no being, no business apart from God. He prospers all these. They are prospered with his presence.

∼

A word on *capital:* When you go to God, close your eyes and think of "I" or "I AM." This "I" is ever one with infinity; it cannot be instructed, healed, enriched, or employed; it is forever at the standpoint of perfection—infinite being. Sometimes we try to bring a human being up to this standard, instead of knowing that the human selfhood fades when we know ourselves as we are. Of this selfhood we can truly know that it is about its Father's business, whole, free.

Your only capital is your principle. This principle is God, undiminished and undiminishing. You can draw on this capital all you wish if you realize that it is principle, infinite, and eternal. Stop personalizing. There is no "my supply" or "your supply;" there is but *one* supply. It is universal, infinite, omnipresent, impersonal, and impartial. There is no "my business" or "your business"; there is only the universal activity of mind expressed as your business and mine. There is but *one* universal harmonious whole and we each express it. There is one principle of mathematics; only one musical scale, and each of us expresses it in the degree that we understand it. How much music can we express? As much as we understand. Music stands in its infinity awaiting expression. It does not select its expression; *we* express it.

To reach out to the one consciousness which never fails to answer, is to us what the "pushing through the throng" was to the woman who touched Jesus' garment and was healed. We must push through the throng because, as he pointed out: "Seek, and ye shall find; knock, and it shall be opened unto you."[5] It is not an asking for supply, or health, but a reaching out to and for that divine consciousness we call Christ, our true being.

Actually, we are already there. We are now spiritual, complete, whole, harmonious, because the image and likeness of God *must* be the exactness of God. However, we need to know this and to remember it every time error tries to talk. I am the embodiment of the qualities and the abundance principle has expressed as me. I am the manifestation of the allness and perfection of its life, its mind, its being. This is why my life, my mind, my being, and my capital or supply, are perfect. They are constituted of the qualities and perfection of principle. While, "I can of mine own self do nothing"[6]—or be nothing—I am the full and complete manifestation of God's completeness, harmony, and perfection. I embody the qualities, activities, character, nature, and abundance of God.

"Ye shall know the truth, and the truth shall make you free."[7] And what is the truth about capital? That it is not personal, that it is of mind and is, therefore, both infinite and omnipresent. Then, only in the degree that we accept the belief that supply is personal or separate from mind, can we suffer from the belief of separation from our supply. When we have learned that supply is impersonal, we will understand the statement that "God is no respecter of persons"[8]—"for he maketh his sun to rise on the evil and on the good, and sendeth rain on the just and on the unjust."[9]

~ 22 ~

HOME

It must become clear to you that as life eternal, you include within yourself the right idea of companionship, friendship, love, and home. Having no qualities undederived from Deity, you have no traits, characteristics, faults, or habits to overcome, destroy, or change. Indeed, you are *now* the all-inclusive activity of mind, life, love. This is true of you and of all men.

It must be equally evident to you that a collection of boards and bricks, even when formed into a structure called a house, does not make a *home.* That which makes a home are the qualities of life which we carry into it. *Atmosphere* makes a home, and atmosphere is created by our thoughts, our consciousness. A joyous home is one expressing the joyous thought and activity of those within its walls.

To build the right sense of home, to secure a right home, to demonstrate home, is to begin within yourself. Ask yourself some questions: "What qualities must I express that will turn a house into a home?" "What qualities constitute the ideal home?" Soon you will realize that cheerfulness, joyousness, cleanliness, orderliness, brightness, hope, consideration of others, forgiveness, co-operation, beauty, grace, love, etc., these qualities expressed by individuals constitute and form that which makes a home.

As you express these in your daily thoughts and acts, you are building within yourself home, and this will externalize itself in what we call our home. Whatever you wish to externalize or experience, must first be built within consciousness, then "consciousness constructs a better body"–a better home.

Regarding civic duties, as students of truth we should be interested in city, state, and country, as well as international affairs. We should strive for betterment in every department of human existence, but I do not think (from our standpoint) that we are justified in directly engaging in crusades. Our spiritual and financial support, plus the moral help we give by attendance at meetings, is as far as it seems wise to go. We should keep our interests free from anything that impedes our spiritual growth.

A period should be reserved each day to work for national and international peace and Christ government, which will in turn be reflected in our home. While it is true that principle governs the entire universe impersonally and impartially, it is likewise true that only in the degree of one's understanding of this truth can he prove it and its manifestation in his human affairs.

A word on *companionship:* Loneliness and all the things that go with it can be joyously dropped if you are willing to abide in the consciousness of truth. You, as an individual, embody in your consciousness every divine idea. The understanding of this enabled Jesus to declare about himself: "I am the way, the truth and the life,"[1] and if you would walk in his way, you must know that this is the truth about you also.

Within your consciousness is embodied the right sense of companionship, fatherhood, motherhood, brotherhood, sonship, and sisterhood. But until you know that these divine ideas are within your consciousness and that, in fact, they constitute your consciousness, you will not receive the full benefit of this truth. Your consciousness of this truth will bring to your experience protection, beauty, harmony, grace, peace, friendship, love, fidelity, and faithfulness, but not until you understand that right *now* you include these within yourself. They, in fact, constitute what is *you.* Then know that: I am love, I am companionship, friendliness, I am completeness, I am allness, because all these divine qualities constitute my consciousness. Dwell in this consciousness of *allness,* of I AM-ness. Take no thought of human circumstance or condition and *let* divine harmony appear.

It is a simple thing to say, "Put not your trust in princes,"[2] but unless we have risen to the spiritual understanding of such truths, we will allow ourselves to be hurt by human experience. As a matter of fact, friend, companion, husband, mate, all of these are divine ideas, but because they appear to human consciousness as men or women, we think of them as such, when they are not. These are never at the mercy of "man, whose breath is in his nostrils," neither can you lose an idea that is embodied within your own consciousness. As you realize you embody them within your own being, you manifest them. You cannot lose health, home, harmony, peace, joy, satisfaction, when you have once seen that they exist as ideas in mind, in your mind.

They are ever-present, because of omnipresence and because of this, they will always be. However, we must gain the true concept of man before we can make progress in our way to scientific understanding. We all know that God is love; that God is mind; that God is all-inclusiveness, but do we remember that "I and the Father are one"[3] and that this "one" does not and cannot mean two? Do we realize that the one consciousness manifests itself, its qualities, as you? Do we remember that you are an individual spiritual consciousness, embodying every quality, activity, and the harmony of mind, life, love? Do we understand that the activity of mind is man; that the faculties of mind are the faculties of man? All action, intelligence, wisdom, is the action of mind, and this action of mind made manifest is man.

All that God is, man must be, because "man is the expression of God's being." When we properly understand this our material needs will be lessened and we will find greater companionship in the kingdom within us, and correspondingly less need for the so-called outer universe. The recognition of the omnipresence of that which *seems* missing, is the power which heals.

Human belief claims that we have problems, but to know that the claim is not our claim, that the belief is not man's, would be to see that man is free, whole, joyous, and harmonious. In the degree that you hold thought steadfastly to this truth, will you find this *allness* revealing itself to you, and so brought into visible expression.

As the Christ, do I need aught? What can I want beside? As the Christ, I *give* all; I feed five thousand, I forgive, I bless, I shine. "Believest thou this."

~ 23 ~

SUPPLY

We would not for a moment consider trying to build a house unless we understood the laws of designing, excavating, building, etc., as well as the local laws of zoning and sanitation. We would not attempt to try a case in court unless we knew the law governing it; nor would we attempt to sail a boat without a knowledge of the laws of navigation. We do, however, attempt to work out our problem of individual supply; we do attempt to demonstrate the availability and abundance of supply without due recognition of the laws which govern it. Many are ignorant of the existence of these laws and believe that a blind faith in some God or power is sufficient to bring about the operation of good in individual experience.

In the absolute there is no need for the working out of the problem of supply. Here there is no demand, because substance is omnipresent and there is no place or time where supply is not. Until we come into this consciousness, the Christ-consciousness, we need to work out our destiny in accord with Scriptural law as found in the scripture of all peoples.

Our first step is the recognition of our true being–our relationship to God. Understanding God to be the one divine universal consciousness, and man to be the individual expression of this consciousness, we find that *all* that the Father hath is mine, that is, all that is embodied in the universal consciousness is embodied in individual consciousness, for they are one. Then, whatsoever things or thoughts we have need of are already a part of our consciousness and will unfold to human apprehension when we are familiar with and apply the law. "Ye shall know the truth, and the truth shall make you free"[1] from the illusion that that which you are seeking is separate and apart from you.

There must be the understanding that the entire universe is embodied in divine mind, and because this is your only mind, all things are already within you. It follows that we are never dependent on any person, place, or condition for anything! Therefore, our next step is to drop all dependence on persons, positions or investments for our supply. This, at first glance, seems preposterous, because the things of the spirit are foolishness to men. "But the natural man receiveth not the things of the spirit of God; for they are foolishness unto him: neither can he know them, because they are spiritually discerned."[2]

A business or a position may seem to be the present channel of our supply. Our students or patients may seem to be our only channels. Housewives may believe their husbands or children are their channels of supply. *But this is not true.* As God, divine consciousness, is the source, so this very consciousness is the channel of supply and indeed, is the *supply* itself.

Try always to look away from your preconceived notion of this. Recognize that all things are embodied in the infinite eternal consciousness, then know that this consciousness is your consciousness. Having dropped all dependence on human and material sources and resources, you will find the continuity of good unfolding in your human experience in the form of the good you need every moment.

While coming into this higher consciousness, obey two important Scriptural injunctions: "The first of the firstfruits of thy land thou shalt bring into the house of the Lord thy God."[3] The way in which to do this should be as the Hebrew Prophet taught: "And this stone, which I have set for a pillar, shall be God's house: and of all that thou shalt give me I will surely give the tenth unto thee."[4]

Recognizing that all that is belongs to God, universal mind, we lay aside from all that which unfolds to us individually a small but definite amount, which we return to the universal, that is, we use it for some purpose not connected with our usual or personal expenditures. We may donate this to any charitable or community cause, we may express gratitude to healer or teacher, but in any event, it must be dedicated to the service of God, good, independent of self or family support. And it must be a "firstfruits"—not a part of that which is left over from our income, but taken out of it when and as it comes in, so that we may use the balance for ourselves and trust God "to give the increase."

Our obedience to these principles enables us to prove that "When all material streams are dried, thy fulness is the same." When we relax the conscious mind's struggle and striving, and let the flow of good pour into us through our spiritual consciousness, we find that we need not fear what mortal man can either give or withhold. We rest in the firm conviction that "The earth is the Lord's and the fulness thereof,"[5] and that *all* that the Father hath is mine; all that exists in the universal is unfolding to the individual.

We come now to perhaps the highest spiritual law of the Bible, the one revealed to us by the Master Christian, Christ Jesus. In the Lord's Prayer we read: "And forgive us our debts as we forgive our debtors."[6] May we not interpret this to mean "forgive us our debts in proportion as we forgive our debtors?" Here you can set your own limitations on your demonstration of good. In *proportion* to *your* forgiving will you receive the blessings of the infinite. We may forgive those who owe us debts of money, and those who owe us debts of love, gratitude, appreciation, or even debts of family or friendly courtesy. But we must forgive. We must live in a constant state of benediction. This is the true forgiveness which releases us from material and mortal obligations.

Some time ago a man came to me in great need of money, being without employment or income. He stated that one of his friends owed him a sum of money which would tide him over the period of lack, and asked: "How would you work on this debt collection?" I told him to forgive the man the debt. Not to write him canceling the debt, as the debt was the other fellow's problem, but to forgive it mentally, and should it never be paid, to think of it no more, not even think unkindly of the so-called debtor. "Drop it from your thought as though it never existed, and *let* divine principle open its channels of supply." He saw the point and turned away from this only visible possible channel of supply to the infinite unseen. The very next week, he earned enough money to support himself for two weeks, and at the end of the second week, he was recalled to his own work from which he had been separated for several years.

~ 24 ~

JESUS FOUNDED NO CHURCH

Jesus did not found any church. He preached in the Hebrew synagogues and by the wayside wherever he went. He taught from the Old Testament, but he corrected many of the religious fallacies of the time and tried to make the Hebrew synagogues less mercenary. He was not in accord with the Hebrew custom of making doctrine, creed, ritual, and ceremony of importance. He did not believe in their long prayers, the sacrificing of animals, etc., but he did believe in worshiping one God; having no idols; remembering that "I can of mine own self do nothing"[1] . . . "but the Father that dwelleth in me, he doeth the works."[2]

He did not believe in the old Jewish God, Jehovah, who sat on a cloud, had a long beard, and wore a white robe. Jesus taught that "the kingdom of God is within you."[3] He did not found a new church, but he added love and understanding to the religion he already knew, and this became the foundation of the Christian Church.

Whereas, the Old Testament taught "an eye for an eye," the new church taught "love your enemies"; "forgive them until seventy times seven." The Hebrews believed in a God who rewarded good and punished evil; the new dispensation said, "Neither do I condemn thee: go, and sin no more."[4] To express it more fully: "For the law was given by Moses, but grace and truth came by Jesus Christ."[5]

Now, it is important that Scientists "agree to disagree" with their former churches, regardless of what the denomination from which they came. Christian Science reaches a higher concept of God than is known in any church.

We have left the personal God of all churches and have accepted impersonal truth, principle, mind, as our God. We have left off the old concept of prayer (that of praying to God for health, wealth, etc.) and we have adopted the higher sense of prayer revealed in *No and Yes,* page 39:17: "true prayer is not asking God for love; it is learning to love, and to include all mankind in one affection. Prayer is the utilization of the love wherewith he loves us. Prayer begets an awakened desire to be and do good. It makes new and scientific discoveries of God, of his goodness and power. It shows us more clearly than we saw before, what we already have and are; and most of all, it shows us what God is. Advancing in this light, we reflect it; and this light reveals the pure mind-pictures, in silent prayer, even as photography grasps the solar light to portray the face of pleasant thought."

Also, we no longer hold to the old concept of man as a mortal, sometimes good, sometimes bad; occasionally healthy, most often ill. We recognize only spiritual man: the manifestation of God's being; the eternal expression of life, incorporeal, and free.

~25~

No Outlined Physical Form

We need to remember that man is not an outlined physical form, nor a finite being surrounded by limitations, but that man is an individual expression of God's being; expressing the infinite good, the eternal harmony, the allness of life, truth and love.

As we dwell on the spiritual nature and character of man, leaving our so-called selfhood out of thought, our divine nature reveals itself in all forms of peace, harmony and perfection. We need to keep constantly in thought that spiritual man is complete and "has not a single quality underived from Deity." Man includes within his own consciousness the freedom and joy of God's being. Man does not sit around waiting to receive these from God, for man is the very expression of these qualities of God. All good is embraced in the divine consciousness which man reflects. This *is*-ness of good is the Christ, truth, revealing the omnipresence of that harmony which may at the moment appear to be absent or apart from us.

Have no fear; trust the Christ as the "divine influence ever-present in human consciousness" which reveals our perfect being. Feel the peace and joy of God flooding your consciousness with his love and his life, and the light will appear.

The question is frequently asked, "How may I know when a healing is complete?" To begin with, we must bear in mind that there can be no actual healing, because there is nothing to be healed. "Spirit is infinite; therefore *spirit is all.* There is no matter."[1] Spirit never needs healing. This is all you need to know. Regardless of appearances, "spirit is all" and spirit does not need healing. There is no "you" outside of mind, so you need no healing. Spirit being all, it is complete. Mind is all, and mind's work is forever complete. You need do no work about this, but you must accept the truth of the completeness of mind. You have no demonstration to make. All action and volition belong to God, and his demonstration (you) was complete from the beginning.

Think less of reading and more of receptivity and reflection. Be receptive to divine ideas and reflect on them. This is the consciousness which forms you anew. God is your life, omnipotent and omnipresent. God is life made manifest *as* you. Now, this life is perfect, complete, harmonious, healthy, and manifests itself as you in all the perfection and harmony of its being. You have no life of your own, and the one you have needs no treating or healing, because his life (your life) is immortal, free.

Mind and its idea, life and its expression, these are *one,* inseparable and indivisible.

Error, evil, disease, discord, exist merely as appearance. But behind this appearance is reality, harmony, peace, joy. Error is a lie about the truth; disease is the lie about harmony and health.

～

We should strive to become conscious of the abundant love and truth which is constantly unfolding from mind—the kingdom within. When we have fully realized that this kingdom is within; that nothing can be added to or taken from the divine being which we are, we will more nearly live the life of abundance: health, wealth, harmony, peace. This is our divine heritage. The joy of the revelation that we are now reflecting infinitely these divine attributes is ours, when we realize that God has not created us; but that he has manifested himself *as* us; that we are his own Selfhood made manifest; that his Selfhood is the only *us* there is.

God has and needs no channels. His Selfhood is directly expressed as his creation. There is in heaven and on earth no one who needs healing, improving, enriching, employing, because we are and always have been God's Selfhood manifested. Truth cannot be brought *to* us. The *belief* that we have needs is the reason we have to contend with problems.

"It is the spirit that quickeneth"–the conscious awareness of truth which reveals to us our true being. However, spiritual consciousness is God, and this is the consciousness of individual being, your own consciousness. It is not something separate or apart from you; something to be gained, earned, won, or sought. There is but one consciousness and it embodies every quality of love, every activity of mind, *all* the harmony of divine being. There is no selfhood apart from God; there is but one life, one being, one mind, and it is your life, your being, your mind.

Nothing can be added to you or taken from you, and into your consciousness nothing can enter that "defileth or maketh a lie." You are about your Father's business. All action, all law, substance, reality, being, cause, and effect are mind, controlling every effect. Cause and effect being one, effect includes *all* that cause is, here and now. Good does not flow from God to you, but it is inherent in mind, and therefore in mind manifest (you), for these are one.

Live every moment in the consciousness of your oneness with your divine principle. "I and my Father are one,"[2] not two. Rejoice in your oneness; that he is the life of your being and the joy of your heart. You are free because he is free. His freedom is your freedom; his life is your life; the harmony of his being is the harmony of your being; his immortality is the infinity of your life.

Give up the sense of personal possession. All that we possess of home, health, wealth, activity, intelligence, belongs to universal mind, life, spirit, which we call God. These "possessions"—faculties and qualities of mind—are expressed *as* the individual you and me, and therefore all that the Father hath and is, is expressed as the individual son. Within you and within me, within individual consciousness is perfection: perfect health, perfect body, mind, beauty, harmony, eternal being. This spiritual self was never born and can neither age nor die. It embraces within itself every requisite by right of this sonship, as joint-heir with Christ.

Only through spiritual sense are we able to discern our true identity as the Christ. Only through spiritual discernment are we able to pierce the veil of illusion and behold the spiritual universe here and now, perfect in its being.

~26~

Universal and Specific Belief

Universal and specific beliefs must be handled until we reach a state of consciousness in which the continuity of good has been realized. Then our mental work will be lessened, as spiritual revelation takes its place.

Outside of Christian Science, humans are born, mature, age, decompose, and die. (All in belief, under the mesmerism of the Adam-dream). In Science, we annul the beliefs and claims of mortal existence one by one, as they appear until, in a measure, the ordinary experiences of mortality leave us untouched.

There comes a time in our experience when spiritual inspiration reveals to individual consciousness a state of being free of mortal conditions and beliefs. Then we no longer live a life of constant mental denial and affirmation, but rather receive constant unfoldments of truth from mind. Sometimes this comes through no other channel than our own thought. It may come from a lecture, or in a published article, or it may be revealed through a statement in metaphysical writings. Regardless of the channel through which it may come, it is mind revealing itself to individual consciousness. Then, be sure that until this light comes, you handle whatever universal beliefs present themselves to you.

As individual consciousness, we contain within ourselves all that is necessary to our well-being. There can be no sense of personal responsibility, when we know that God, divine love, completely provides within us all that is necessary for our unfoldment. As we give up personal responsibility, we receive divine strength, desire, and ability to help all those who for the moment may seem to need us. It is the divine "I or us" that fills the need of the patient, families or friends. Never do they need the personal you or me.

As to our being ready to work from the point of spiritual revelation, that is never a matter for human decision. You just work as it comes to you to work, remembering that the human mind is not the healer; that mind does reveal itself to the listening ear. God always reveals itself in the silence of our being, when the senses are still.

~27~

MALPRACTICE

I want to digress today in order to clear up a couple of misunderstandings, which are continually causing difficulties to working Scientists.

There is a very prevalent belief that hate, envy, jealousy, etc., coming at us through the thoughts of others, can cause physical distress, sickness, or even death. In other words, it is believed that the evil thoughts of others can adversely affect us. It must be thoroughly understood that this is not so. Thoughts of others, even when directed at us, ignorantly or maliciously, have no power to harm us. Nothing from without can enter that "defileth, . . . or maketh a lie."

"Christian Science translates mind, God, to mortals. It is the infinite calculus defining the line, plane, space, and fourth dimension of spirit. It absolutely refutes the amalgamation, transmigration, absorption, or annihilation of individuality. It shows the impossibility of transmitting human ills, or evil, from one individual to another; that all true thoughts revolve in God's orbits; they come from God and return to him,—and untruths belong not to his creation, therefore these are null and void."[1] "What can there be besides infinity? Nothing! Therefore the Science of Good calls evil *nothing*. Here is where Christian Science sticks to its text and other systems of religion abandon their own logic. Here also is found the pith of the basal statement, the cardinal point in Christian Science, that matter and evil (including all inharmony, sin, disease, death) are *unreal.*"[2] "What is the cardinal point of the difference in my metaphysical system? This: that by *knowing the unreality of disease, sin, and death,* you demonstrate the allness of God. This difference wholly separates my system from all others. The reality of these so-called existences I deny, because they are not to be found in God, and this system is built on Him as the sole cause."[3] "Animal magnetism, hypnotism, etc., are disarmed by the practitioner who excludes from his own consciousness, and that of his patients, all sense of the realism of any other cause or effect save that which cometh from God."[4]

Evil thoughts, when *we* entertain them, may cause temporary ill. This is because we are accepting a presence or power apart from God. This does not mean that erroneous thoughts cause disease, because the revelation of truth is that there is no disease, but when mesmerism blinds us even temporarily to entertaining thoughts of hate, fear, revenge, doubt, suspicion, envy, greed, etc., we must not be surprised if it brings a temporary penalty. Let us learn then that we must not fear the thoughts of other people, but must learn to watch the thoughts that we express.

Do not, however, go to the other extreme and fear a result from every negative thought you think. That is sheer nonsense. One would have to indulge an awful lot of devilish thinking for it to produce any harmful result, because most human thinking has no power for evil and no power for good.

This leads to the second misconception: namely, that there is a divine love somewhere that is going to meet your human need. Just as there are no evil thoughts outside of you that will harm you, so there is no divine love outside of you that is going to bless you. Many have been fooled by misinterpreting Mrs. Eddy's grand statement: "Divine Love always has met and always will meet every human need."[5]

Always remember that it is the divine love *you* give forth that meets your human need. If there is any harm from evil thinking it is only from the evil thoughts you permit to go out from you, and likewise if love is to meet your human need it is only the divine love you show forth.

Mrs. Eddy makes it clear that "the mind of the individual only can produce a result upon his body,"[6] and the "mind of the individual" is God. You will remember the statement of Mrs. Eddy: "Mystery, miracle, sin, and death will disappear when it becomes fairly understood that the divine mind controls man and man has no mind but God."[7]

Therefore the only result this mind can produce is good. Any seeming result from "wrong thinking" can be immediately dispelled through the recognition of its nothingness, its existence merely as mirage without substance, law, reality, cause or effect.

The truth we entertain in consciousness produces the real lasting effects upon our bodies; the impersonal universal love we give outlet to meets our every human need.

~28~

RICHARD DAVIS LECTURE

The Richard Davis lecture in the Christian Science Monitor of December 3, 1935, gives us much to think about. He stated: "When John declared that God is Love . . . he was not endeavoring to formulate a concept of Deity based on sentiment or emotion." This statement of Mr. Davis needs careful study and application.

When we are tempted to wonder if we must *do* something or *think* something to help our demonstration, we might dwell on Mr. Davis' remark: "Man is not called upon to enforce the law of Love, for it is its own enforcement; but he does become conscious of its existence and experiences the revelation in his own consciousness of its action." Too often we strive to work out our own destiny, and regarding this he says: "The human sense struggles to work out its own destiny even while divine Love waits to fulfill every aspiration soaring toward good."

Repeatedly I have referred you to this statement in *Science and Health* that there is "a divine influence ever present in human consciousness,"[1] which we understand to be the Christ, able and willing to do all things for you. Of this, Mr. Davis says: "The Christ in your consciousness will govern every act of your being. It will make you a good man and a successful one, and, if you accept it fully, it will glorify your being."

Our message finds support in this paragraph: "Christian Science declares that there is nothing wrong with the real man. The process of Christian Science treatment is not that of changing a sick man into a healthy one, or a diseased body into a well one. God's man is already well and free. It is our privilege to see and know it." And to support this, he quotes from *Miscellany:* "You can never demonstrate spirituality until you declare yourself to be immortal and understand that you are so. Christian Science is absolute; it is neither behind the point of perfection nor advancing towards it; it is at this point and must be practiced therefrom. Unless you fully perceive that you are the child of God, hence perfect, you have no Principle to demonstrate and no rule for its demonstration."[2]

Thus does he touch on the subject of fear: "Fear comes to every one of us as a temptation to believe in evil as a real power, as an active force in creation . . . is the almighty, the omnipotent, confronted with another power called evil? If so, almighty is a misnomer. All the fear that has ever existed in human thought through all the ages has never affected in the slightest degree the orderly government of the universe. Now certainly, then, may we rest in the assurance that the unseen, yet ever-operating law of love is wisely, tenderly, governing all, and that there is nothing to fear."

Very often we hear the expression, "the fear of fear." This comes from the belief that one's conscious fear produces the thing he fears. Regardless of what you consciously fear, it cannot hurt you. It has *no* power. This is true of the thing you fear as well as the fear itself, regardless of the extent of the fear.

Conscious fear is an effect, in exactly the same way that sickness or poverty is, and effects can never become cause. Therefore, they can never produce *anything.*

God, good, is the only cause and creator, and there can be no effects from any other cause. Study this quotation from *Science and Health:* "There is but one primal cause. Therefore there can be no effect from any other cause, and there can be no reality in aught which does not proceed from this great and only cause."[3]

Fortified with the knowledge that God, life, mind, spirit, is the only cause, you can readily understand that neither germs, accidents, losses, sins, nor fears can act as cause. Therefore, these conditions being devoid of power as cause, they can neither have nor result in any effect.

Keep firmly in mind that good has no opposite and no opposition. Ponder frequently the quotation given above, as well as: "To grasp the reality and order of being in its Science, you must begin by reckoning God as the divine Principle of all that really is. Spirit, Life, Truth, Love, combine as one,–and are the Scriptural names for God. All substance, intelligence, wisdom, being, immortality, cause, and effect belong to God. These are His attributes, the eternal manifestations of the infinite divine Principle, Love. No wisdom is wise but His wisdom; no truth is true, no love is lovely, no life is Life but the divine; no good is, but the good God bestows."[4] "Neither disease itself, sin, nor fear has the power to cause disease or a relapse."[5] ". . . Spirit is *spiritual* consciousness alone. Hence this spiritual consciousness can form nothing unlike itself, Spirit, and Spirit is the only creator. The material atom is an outlined falsity of consciousness, which can gather additional evidence of consciousness and life only as it adds lie to lie. This process it names material attraction, and endows with the double capacity of creator and creation. From the beginning this lie was the false witness against the fact that Spirit is All, beside which there is no other existence." [6]

~29~

WHAT OF DEATH?

Drink with Me this cup of inspiration,
Sip this wine, revealing Life divine,
Walk with Me in the shade of revelation,
For I AM Life.
Can Life do aught but live?
Can the sun do less than shine?
Or the stars withhold their gleam?
Is not the breath you breathe
The same I breathed into your being?
    Shall God withdraw Himself?
Come with Me for just a moment,
Away from city streets, and even country lanes.
Away from the Babel of tongues, and the
    strain of thought,
To where the beckoning finger of Love
    Points the Way.
And rest awhile in the consciousness of
    My presence,
Illuming the dark recesses of fancy,
So that the Light of Truth may
Open your hearts to the concept of
The gift of God,—eternal Life.

There is no death. Death is but illusion. It is the
terminal of the belief that man is born. To realize the

nothingness of death, we must start with the understanding of the unreality of that which we call birth. This understanding evolves from the discernment of the Master's statement: "Before Abraham was, I AM."[1] Man can no more be conscious of death than he can be conscious of birth. There can be no more awareness of passing on than there can be of coming, for "Lo, I AM with you always."[2]

Abstract metaphysical statements offer no consolation to those separated from loved ones. Platitudes can never replace the "peace be still" of the touch of Christ-like hands. Heavy hearts are lifted only as the gaze rests upon the vision of eternal life, and this forever radiating as man.

Our belief that one has passed on does not change him. Jesus returned in the same form and body in spite of the belief held by those who witnessed the crucifixion, that he had died. Our beliefs do not affect those who seem to have left our midst. Their lives continue in uninterrupted rhythm, though, to them, it is as if we remained behind while they go on.

You have never known death thus far and you never will. Your only remembrance is of life and living, and so it will ever be. How proud we felt on graduation day, when we had reached that great climax. Yet, how eagerly we looked forward to the greater experiences that were ahead of us. Did we think it necessary to die in order to go on to greater heights? Every progressive step in life is a higher one on to freedom from the limitations of immaturity and restrictions. The only death there can be is the death of the beliefs of limitations.

Man is the offspring of God. Human birth is a false concept of the orderly unfoldment or development in consciousness of individual experience. Death is but the belief that consciousness has withdrawn itself from its own manifested being, and this can no more be so than that the sun can withdraw its warmth and light from its own rays.

The body is the externalization of thought, and manifests the various beliefs which we accept. When we have overcome the belief in death the body can no longer succumb to it. Then death is not to be destroyed as a condition of body, but overcome in individual thought as a lie about life.

> I would lead you to a garden
> Where the view is ever fair,
> Where the light of Life is shining,
> And the heart is free from care.
> Here my Master rests, and teaches
> Of the glories of His Way.
> Here the wearied lay their burdens
> And rejoice to see His Day.

~ 30 ~

WAR

Of all the so-called errors on earth, war is the belief most likely to ensnare the Christian Scientist into accepting an illusion as reality. The reason for this is that there always seem to be two sides; one on the right side defending "democracy," "modern society," "Christianity," "freedom," while the other, on the wrong side, would destroy these precious gifts from God to man (which gifts, it would seem, God is not able to preserve without the help of defenders). I am not referring exclusively to either of the "World Wars" because these same conditions have existed in all wars throughout the ages.

Christian Scientists cannot say, "A thousand shall fall at thy (my) side, and ten thousand at thy (my) right hand; but it shall not come nigh thee (me),"[1] unless they see through the snare of a right side and a wrong side and realize that there is no such condition as right and wrong because there is no war, no error, no sin, disease or death:

God *is* all; God *is* omnipresent; God *is* the only life and being, and in this life which is *one* there can be no conflicting forces, energies, or desires.

Christian Science teachers and practitioners throughout the world, daily assure their students and their patients that there is no disease; that the appearance of such is but the false testimony of human sense; that they are not to fear error nor believe in its reality or power. They are taught and they teach that God is the only mind. Shall they not be consistent and remember that, as this divine mind is the universal mind, and therefore the mind of individual being, there is no lack of intelligence and love in this mind and therefore these qualities of love, intelligence, harmony and peace are the actual and only states of being here and now, regardless of human testimony to the contrary.

Only in the degree that we, as disciples of truth and love, maintain in our consciousness this truth of being, shall we be lifted up so as to "draw all men unto me," and thereby cause all men to see and be at peace.

> "I know no life divided,
>   O Lord of life, from Thee;
> In Thee is life provided
>   For all mankind and me;
> I know no death, O Father
>   Because I live in Thee;
> Thy life it is that frees us
>   From death eternally."
>   – *Christian Science Hymnal*

Does this indicate that there is a person, a power, an ideology, or a system of government whereby the life, well-being, or continuity of good is threatened? "In thee is life provided;"–"thy life it is that frees us." This life in God and of God is not at the mercy of "man whose breath is in his nostrils." Therefore, "I will not fear what flesh (man) can do unto me."[2]

Let us be sure that we are not ensnared with the belief that there is warfare between good and evil, God and the devil. There is no evil. There is no channel, no target, no victim of evil. God *is* all. God is "all-in-all." God is the principle of all being and there can be no lack of principle anywhere or in any being. In the infinitude of God's being there can be only the eternal presence of his love, his life, his wisdom, his guidance, and this truth, enthroned in individual consciousness, is the savior and protection from the belief in a presence and power apart from God.

The moment we accept the belief that there is greed, mad ambition, personal will, ignorance, and that we need to battle these, war with them and set up elaborate defenses against them, we are on the same level of thought with this evil. This should not in any way prevent those who accept evil as real from having armies and navies, and even having defensive war itself, but it does mean that we, as disciples of truth, have reached the understanding of Christ sufficiently to say, "Fear ye not, stand still, and see the salvation of the Lord"[3]–"for the battle is not yours, but God's."[4] It means that we have arrived at a state of consciousness which does not war with error, does not argue with evil, but recognizes that there is no error because "as in heaven, so on earth, God is omnipotent, supreme."[5]

Jesus said, "Put up again thy sword into his place: for all they that take the sword shall perish with the sword."[6] To take up the sword in defense, is to acknowledge the presence of an enemy, a power, and a presence apart from God; it is to believe in the reality of right and wrong, good and evil. This is a snare and a delusion.

As a Christian Scientist and a member of the U. S. Marine Corps in World War I, I was troubled in doing my daily "protective work" because it seemed inconsistent to believe that I could seek and receive the protection of God for myself, when I was so heavily armed with implements of war from which any so-called enemy coming near me was bound to suffer. Seeking light on this point I was led to the words of Jesus: "Neither pray I for these alone, but for all."[7]–I could go no further because I saw clearly that my protective work was the realization and understanding that all men are "the children of God: And if children, then heirs: heirs of God, and joint-heirs with Christ,"[8] that *all* men abide in his life –"Hid with Christ in God"[9]–"in the secret place of the Most High."[10] In my nearly two years of service, I was never called on to fire at any man, nor to be fired upon. Ever since then I have realized the universality of God, good, in whom is no evil and who is "of purer eyes than to behold evil, and canst not look on iniquity."[11]

The First Commandment is, "Thou shalt have no other gods before me,"[12] which we understand to mean: thou shalt not believe in any power, or presence other than God. "God is everywhere, and nothing apart from Him is present or has power."[13] Then where or what is this evil to be fought or destroyed except in the belief that God is not everywhere and that something apart from him *is* present and has power? "Choose you this day whom ye will serve."[14]

Scriptural References
and Notes

All Bible references are from the King James translation of the Bible.

All references from the writings of Mary Baker Eddy are from the editions current at the time that this work was originally published in 1949.

The abbreviations used in the footnotes are as follows:

S. & H.	*Science and Health with Key to the Scriptures*
Mis.	*Miscellaneous Writings*
No.	*No and Yes*
Ret.	*Retrospection and Introspection*
Hea.	*Christian Healing*
My.	*First Church of Christ Scientist and Miscellany*
Un.	*Unity of Good*

Chapter 1
1. John 19:11
2. S. & H. 390:7–9
3. S. & H. 203:7–8
4. S. & H. 588:11
5. S. & H. 17:2–3
6. John 1:3
7. Genesis 1:31
8. S. & H. 411:20–21
9. Ezekiel 18:2–3
10. S. & H. 151:21–23
11. S. & H. 207:20–23
12. S. & H. 415:1–3
13. S. & H. 419:10–12
14. Mis. 93:6, 21
15. No. 10:27–3
16. Luke 17:21

Chapter 1 (Continued)
17. Mark 11:24
18. Matthew 6:33
19. John 2:19
20. Matthew 6:25

Chapter 2
1. S. & H. 209:31–32
2. 1 John 3:1
3. John 8:32
4. Matthew 16:13
5. Matthew 16:16
6. John 14:6
7. John 8:12
8. Isaiah 2:22
9. John 10:30
10. John 14:9

Chapter 2 (Continued)
11. John 8:12
12. Matthew 5:14
13. John 6:69

Chapter 3
1. Ret. 93:3–4
2. John 7:24
3. Matthew 25:29
4. Isaiah 55:11
5. John 5:30
6. John 5:17
7. Acts 17:28
8. S. & H. 126:8–9
9. I Corinthians 16:13
10. John 10:30
11. John 14:6
12. John 11:25
13. John 8:12
14. Matthew 6:33
15. John 14:6
16. John 11:25
17. John 6:35

Chapter 4
1. Revelation 22:5
2. Genesis 1:3
3. Job 26:7
4. John 18:36
5. S. & H. 505:27–28
6. John 18:36
7. S. & H. 231:16
8. John 16:33
9. Luke 15:31
10. S. & H. 14:25–26
11. Luke 15:31

Chapter 5
1. John 10:30
2. Colossians 3:4

Chapter 5 (Continued)
3. Daniel 6:22
4. John 14:30
5. John 7:24
6. S. & H. 583:10–11
7. Mis. 185:7–11
8. S. & H. 591:5–7

Chapter 6
1. Isaiah 26:3
2. S. & H. 468:10–11
3. S. & H. 476:32–4
4. Exodus 3:14
5. John 10:30
6. Matthew 5:6
7. S. & H. 470:23-24
8. Genesis 1:27
9. Ret. 93:3-4

Chapter 7
1. S. & H. 379:6
2. Luke 15:31
3. Luke 17:21
4. Romans 8:17
5. Acts 17:28
6. John 2:19
7. Ezekiel 18:2,3
8. S. & H. 468:10-11
9. S. & H. 475:14-15, 19-20
10. John 9:2
11. John 9:3
12. Joshua 1:5
13. Matthew 12:39
14. Mark 16:17
15. Matthew 19:17
16. I John 3:2
17. II Corinthians 3:6

Chapter 8
1. S. & H. 2:8

Chapter 8 (Continued)
2. S. & H. 2:23-25
3. S. & H. 2:31-2
4. S. & H. 3:4-5
5. John 5:30
6. John 14:10
7. Genesis 1:1,31
8. John 18:36
9. Luke 17:21

Chapter 9
1. Philippians 2:5
2. John 5:30
3. Matthew 19:17
4. Philippians 2:5
5. Mis. 101:31
6. Hea. 6:21-22

Chapter 10
1. John 18:36
2. I Samuel 3:10
3. II Kings 6:17
4. Job 32:8
5. Romans 1:25
6. Zechariah 4:6

Chapter 11
1. John 2:19
2. Matthew 6:27
3. Luke 12:22,27
4. Psalm 91:10
5. S. & H. 254:19-20
6. S. & H. 324:4-5
7. Matthew 5:6
8. S. & H. 209:31-32
9. Matthew 6:27
10. John 12:45
11. I John 3:2
12. Romans 8:17
13. John 18:36

Chapter 12
1. S. & H. 470:23-24
2. S. & H. 471:18-19
3. S. & H. 476:32-2
4. S. & H. 297:32
5. I John 4:4
6. S. & H. 218:24-25
7. S. & H. 17:2-3
8. Revelation 3:20
9. I John 4:20

Chapter 13
1. S. & H. 319:20
2. Matthew 16:13
3. Exodus 3:14
4. Isaiah 55:11
5. John 12:45
6. John 6:63
7. John 14:12
8. Daniel 7:13, 14, 27
9. Matthew 9:6
10. Luke 6:5
11. John 12:35
12. Ezekiel 2:1
13. Matthew 16:13, 16
14. Hea. 6:21-22
15. John 5:30
16. John 14:10
17. Matthew 6:27
18. Luke 12:22, 30, 32
19. Isaiah 60:1
20. John 11:43
21. Luke 5:24
22. Isaiah 2:22
23. John 10:30
24. Exodus 20:3
25. John 1:4
26. S. & H. 393:29-30

Chapter 14
1. John 19:10
2. John 19:11

197

Chapter 15
1. John 12:45
2. Zechariah 4:6
3. Isaiah 30:15
4. Matthew 6:33

Chapter 17
1. S. & H. 368:24-26
2. S. & H. 181:1-2
3. Zechariah 4:6
4. S. & H. 327:29

Chapter 18
1. S. & H. 390:7-9
2. John 8:32

Chapter 19
1. Matthew 6:33
2. Philippians 4:8
3. James 1:17
4. John 6:37
5. Luke 12:22, 26

Chapter 20
1. Ecclesiastes 3:14
2. S. & H. 264:20
3. John 14:6
4. John 11:25
5. John 12:45
6. John 5:18
7. Philippians 2:6
8. II Corinthians 6:17
9. John 1:3
10. Genesis 1:31
11. S. & H. 468:9-11
12. S. & H. 379:6-7
13. Ret. 93:3-4

Chapter 21
1. John 8:32

Chapter 21 (Continued)
2. Hebrews 12:1
3. John 4:35
4. S. & H. 507:28-29
5. Matthew 7:7
6. John 5:30
7. John 8:32
8. Acts 10:34
9. Matthew 5:45

Chapter 22
1. John 14:6
2. Psalm 146:3
3. John 10:30

Chapter 23
1. John 8:32
2. I Corinthians 2:14
3. Exodus 23:19
4. Genesis 28:22
5. Psalm 24:1
6. Matthew 6:12

Chapter 24
1. John 5:30
2. John 14:10
3. Luke 17:21
4. John 8:11
5. John 1:17

Chapter 25
1. My. 357:22-23
2. John 10:30

Chapter 27
1. Mis. 23:10-19
2. Mis. 27:1-2, 7-12
3. Un. 9:27-5
4. My. 364:9-13
5. S. & H. 494:10-11

Chapter 27 (Continued)
 6. Hea. 6:21-22
 7. S. & H. 319:17

Chapter 28
 1. S. & H. XI:16-17
 2. My. 242:3-10
 3. S. & H. 207:20-23
 4. S. & H. 275:10
 5. S. & H. 419:10-11
 6. Un. 35:24-6

Chapter 29
 1. John 8:58
 2. Matthew 28:20

Chapter 30
 1. Psalm 91:7
 2. Psalm 56:4
 3. Exodus 14:13
 4. II Chronicles 20:15
 5. S. & H. 17:2-3
 6. Matthew 26:52
 7. John 17:20
 8. Romans 8:17
 9. Colossians 3:3
 10. Psalm 91:1
 11. Habakkuk 1:13
 12. Exodus 20:3
 13. S. & H. 473:8-10
 14. Joshua 24:15